The Blue Bird:
A Fairy Play in Six Acts

Maurice Maeterlinck

Contents

THE BLUE BIRD 7
TRANSLATOR'S NOTE 9
COSTUMES 10
ACT I 13
ACT II 39
SCENE I.--At the FAIRY'S 39
SCENE 2.--The Land of Memory 50
ACT III. 65
SCENE 1.--The Palace of NIGHT. 65
SCENE 2.--The Forest. 85
ACT IV 108
SCENE 1.--Before the Curtain. 108
SCENE 2.--The Palace of Happiness. 111
ACT V 132
SCENE I.--Before the Curtain. 132
SCENE 2.--The Graveyard. 135
SCENE 3.--The Kingdom of the Future. 141
ACT VI 167
SCENE I.--The Leave-taking. 167
SCENE 2.--The Awakening. 179

THE BLUE BIRD:
A FAIRY PLAY IN SIX ACTS

BY

Maurice Maeterlinck

THE BLUE BIRD
A Fairy Play in Six Acts
BY
MAURICE MAETERLINCK

CHARACTERS

TYLTYL
MYTYL
LIGHT
THE FAIRY BERYLUNE
NEIGHBOUR BERLINGOT
DADDY TYL
MUMMY TYL
GAFFER TYL (Dead)
GRANNY TYL (Dead)
TYLTYL'S BROTHERS AND SISTERS (Dead)
TIME
NIGHT
NEIGHBOUR BERLINGOT'S LITTLE DAUGHTER
TYLO, THE DOG
TYLETTE, THE CAT
BREAD
SUGAR
FIRE
WATER
MILK

THE WOLF
THE PIG
THE OX
THE COW
THE BULL
THE SHEEP
THE COCK
THE RABBIT
THE HORSE
THE ASS
THE OAK
THE ELM
THE BEECH
THE LIME-TREE
THE FIR-TREE
THE CYPRESS
THE BIRCH
THE CHESTNUT-TREE
THE IVY
THE POPLAR
THE WILLOW
STARS, SICKNESSES, SHADES, LUXURIES, HAPPINESSES, JOYS, ETC.

TRANSLATOR'S NOTE

A new act appears for the first time in this edition and is inserted as Act IV--Palace of Happiness. It has been specially written for the Christmas revival of *The Blue Bird* at the Haymarket Theatre, where it will take the place of the Forest Scene (Act III., Scene 2). In the printed version, however, the Forest Scene is retained; and in this and all later editions the play will consist of six acts instead of five.

ALEXANDER TEIXEIRA DE MATTOS.
CHELSEA, 14 *November*, 1910.

COSTUMES

TYLTYL wears the dress of Hop o' my Thumb in Perrault's Tales. Scarlet knickerbockers, pale-blue jacket, white stockings, tan shoes.

MYTYL is dressed like Gretel or Little Red Riding-hood.

LIGHT.--The "moon-coloured" dress in Perrault's **Peau d'ane;** that is to say, pale gold shot with silver, shimmering gauzes, forming a sort of rays, etc. Neo-Grecian or Anglo-Grecian (a la Walter Crane) or even more or less Empire style: a high waist, bare arms, etc. Head-dress: a sort of diadem or even a light crown.

THE FAIRY BERYLUNE and NEIGHBOUR BERLINGOT.--The traditional dress of the
poor women in fairy-tales. If desired, the transformation of the Fairy into a princess in Act I may be omitted.

DADDY TYL, MUMMY TYL, GAFFER TYL and GRANNY TYL.--The traditional costume
of the German wood-cutters and peasants in Grimm's Tales.

TYLTYL'S BROTHERS AND SISTERS.--Different forms of the Hop-o'-my-Thumb
costume.

TIME.--Traditional dress of Time: a wide black or dark-blue cloak, a streaming white beard, scythe and hour-glass.

NIGHT.--Ample black garments, covered with mysterious stars and "shot" with
reddish-brown reflections. Veils, dark poppies, etc.

THE NEIGHBOUR'S LITTLE GIRL.--Bright fair hair; a long white frock.

THE DOG,--Red dress-coat, white breeches, top-boots, a shiny hat. The costume suggests that of John Bull.

THE CAT.--The costume of Puss In Boots: powdered wig, three-cornered hat, violet or sky-blue coat, dress-sword, etc.

N.B.--The heads of the DOG and the CAT should be only discreetly animalised.

THE LUXURIES.--Before the transformation: wide, heavy mantles in red and yellow brocade; enormous fat jewels, etc. After the transformation: chocolate or coffee-coloured tights, giving the impression of unadorned dancing-jacks.

THE HAPPINESSES OF THE HOME.--Dresses of various colours, or, if preferred,
costumes of peasants, shepherds, wood-cutters and so on, but idealised and interpreted fairy-fashion.

THE GREAT JOYS.--As stated in the text, shimmering dresses in soft and subtle shades: rose-awakening, water's-smile, amber-dew, blue-of-dawn, etc.

MATERNAL LOVE.--Dress very similar to the dress worn by Light, that is to say, supple and almost transparent veils, as of a Greek statue, and, in so far as possible, white. Pearls and other stones as rich and numerous as may be desired, provided that they do not break the pure and candid harmony of the whole.

BREAD.--A rich pasha's dress. An ample crimson silk or velvet gown. A huge turban. A scimitar. An enormous stomach, red and puffed-out cheeks.

SUGAR.--A silk gown, cut like that of a eunuch in a seraglio, half blue and half white, to suggest the paper wrapper of a sugar-loaf. Eunuch's headdress.

FIRE.--Red tights, a vermilion cloak, with changing reflections, lined with gold. An aigrette of iridescent flames.

WATER.--A pale-blue or bluish-green dress, with transparent reflections and effects of rippling or trickling gauze, Neo-Grecian or Anglo-Grecian style. but fuller and more voluminous than that of LIGHT. Head-dress of aquatic flowers and seaweed.

THE ANIMALS.--Popular or peasant costumes.

THE TREES.--Dresses of different shades of green or the colour of the trunks of trees. Distinctive attributes in the shape of leaves or branches by which they can be recognised.

ACT I

The Wood-cutter's Cottage

The stage represents the interior of a wood-cutter's cottage, simple and rustic in appearance, but in no way poverty-stricken. A recessed fireplace containing the dying embers of a wood-fire. Kitchen utensils, a cupboard, a bread-pan, a grandfather's clock, a spinning-wheel, a water-tap, etc. On a table, a lighted lamp. At the foot of the cupboard, on either side, a DOG *and a* CAT *lie sleeping, rolled up, each with his nose in his tail. Between them stands a large blue-and-white sugar-loaf. On the wall hangs a round cage containing a turtle-dove. At the back, two windows, with*

closed inside shutters. Under one of the windows, a stool. On the left is the front door, with a big latch to it. On the right, another door. A ladder leads up to a loft. On the right also are two little children's cots, at the head of which are two chains, with clothes carefully folded on them. When the curtain rises, TYLTYL *and* MYTYL *are sound asleep in their cots,* MUMMY TYL *tucks them in, leans over them, watches them for a moment as they sleep and beckons to* DADDY TYL, who thrusts his head through the half-open door. MUMMY TYL *lays a finger on her lips, to impose silence upon him, and then goes out to the right, on tiptoe, after first putting out the lamp. The scene remains in darkness for a moment. Then a light, gradually increasing in intensity, filters in through the shutters. The lamp on the table lights again of itself, but its light is of a different colour than when* MUMMY TYL *extinguished it. The two* CHILDREN *appear to wake and sit up in bed*.

TYLTYL
Mytyl?

MYTYL
Tyltyl?

TYLTYL
Are you asleep?

MYTYL
Are you?...

TYLTYL
No; how can I be asleep when I'm talking to you?

MYTYL
Say, is this Christmas Day?...

TYLTYL
Not yet; not till to-morrow. But Father Christmas won't bring us anything this year....

MYTYL
Why not?

TYLTYL
I heard mummy say that she couldn't go to town to tell him ... But he will come next year....

MYTYL
Is next year far off?...

TYLTYL
A good long while.... But he will come to the rich children to-night....

MYTYL
Really?...

TYLTYL
Hullo!... Mummy's forgotten to put out the lamp!... I've an idea!...

MYTYL
What?...

TYLTYL
Let's get up....

MYTYL
But we mustn't....

TYLTYL
Why, there's no one about.... Do you see the shutters?...

MYTYL
Oh, how bright they are!...

TYLTYL
It's the lights of the party.

MYTYL
What party?...

TYLTYL
The rich children opposite. It's the Christmas-tree. Let's open the shutters....

MYTYL
Can we?...

TYLTYL
Of course; there's no one to stop us.... Do you hear the music?... Let us get up....

(The two CHILDREN *get up, run to one of the windows, climb on to the stool and throw back the shutters. A bright light fills the room. The* CHILDREN *look out greedily*.)

TYLTYL
We can see everything!...

MYTYL (who can hardly find room on the stool)
I can't....

TYLTYL
It's snowing!... There's two carriages, with six horses each!...

MYTYL
There are twelve little boys getting out!...

TYLTYL
How silly you are!... They're little girls....

MYTYL
They've got knickerbockers....

TYLTYL
What do you know?... Don't push so!...

MYTYL
I never touched you.

TYLTYL (who is taking up the whole stool)
You're taking up all the room...

MYTYL
Why, I have no room at all!...

TYLTYL
Do be quiet! I see the tree!...

MYTYL
What tree?...

TYLTYL
Why, the Christmas-tree!... You're looking at the wall!...

MYTYL
I'm looking at the wall because I've got no room....

TYLTYL (giving her a miserly little place on the stool)
There!... Will that do?... Now you're better off than I!... I say, what lots and lots of lights!...

MYTYL
What are those people doing who are making such a noise?...

TYLTYL
They're the musicians.

MYTYL
Are they angry?...

TYLTYL
No; but it's hard work.

MYTYL
Another carriage with white horses!...

TYLTYL
Be quiet!... And look!...

MYTYL
What are those gold things there, hanging from the branches?

TYLTYL
Why, toys, to be sure!... Swords, guns, soldiers, cannons....

MYTYL
And dolls; say, are there any dolls?...

TYLTYL
Dolls?... That's too silly; there's no fun in dolls....

MYTYL
And what's that all round the table?....

TYLTYL
Cakes and fruit and tarts....

MYTYL
I had some once when I was little....

TYLTYL
So did I; it's nicer than bread, but they don't give you enough....

MYTYL
They've got plenty over there.... The whole table's full.... Are they going to eat them?...

TYLTYL
Of course; what else would they do with them?...

MYTYL
Why don't they eat them at once?...

TYLTYL
Because they're not hungry....

MYTYL (stupefied with astonishment)
Not hungry?... Why not?...

TYLTYL
Well, they eat whenever they want to....

MYTYL (incredulously)
Every day?...

TYLTYL
They say so....

MYTYL
Will they eat them all?... Will they give any away?...

TYLTYL
To whom?...

MYTYL
To us....

TYLTYL
They don't know us....

MYTYL
Suppose we asked them....

TYLTYL
We mustn't.

MYTYL
Why not?...

TYLTYL
Because it's not right.

MYTYL (clapping her hands)
Oh, how pretty they are!...

TYLTYL (rapturously)
And how they're laughing and laughing!...

MYTYL
And the little ones dancing!...

TYLTYL
Yes, yes; let's dance too!... (They stamp their feet for joy on the stool.)

MYTYL
Oh, what fun!...

TYLTYL
They're getting the cakes!... They can touch them!... They're eating, they're eating, they're eating!...

MYTYL
The tiny ones, too!... They've got two, three, four apiece!...

TYLTYL (drunk with delight)
Oh, how lovely!... Oh, how lovely, how lovely!...

MYTYL (counting imaginary cakes)
I've got twelve!...

TYLTYL
And I four times twelve!... But I'll give you some....

(A knock at the door of the cottage.)

TYLTYL (suddenly quieted and frightened)
What's that?...

MYTYL (scared)
It's Daddy!...

(As they hesitate before opening the door, the big latch is seen to rise of itself, with a grating noise; the door half opens to admit a little old woman dressed in green with a red hood on her head. She is humpbacked and lame and near-sighted; her nose and chin meet; and she walks bent on a stick. She is obviously a fairy.)

THE FAIRY
Have you the grass here that sings or the bird that is blue?...

TYLTYL
We have some grass, but it can't sing....

MYTYL
Tyltyl has a bird.

TYLTYL
But I can't give it away....

THE FAIRY
Why not?...

TYLTYL
Because it's mine.

THE FAIRY
That's a reason, no doubt. Where is the bird?...

TYLTYL (pointing to the cage)
In the cage....

THE FAIRY (putting on her glasses to examine the bird)
I don't want it; it's not blue enough. You will have to go and find me the one I want.

TYLTYL
But I don't know where it is....

THE FAIRY
No more do I. That's why you must look for it. I can do without the grass that sings, at a pinch; but I must absolutely have the blue bird. It's for my little girl, who is very ill.

TYLTYL
What's the matter with her?...

THE FAIRY
We don't quite know; she wants to be happy....

TYLTYL
Really?...

THE FAIRY
Do you know who I am?...

TYLTYL
You're rather like our neighbour, Madame Berlingot....

THE FAIRY (growing suddenly angry)
Not a bit!... There's not the least likeness!... This is intolerable!... I am the Fairy Berylune....

TYLTYL
Oh! Very well....

THE FAIRY
You will have to start at once.

TYLTYL
Are you coming with us?

THE FAIRY
I can't, because I put on the soup this morning and it always boils over if I leave it for more than an hour.... (Pointing successively to the ceiling, the chimney and the window) Will you go out this way, or that way, or that way?...

TYLTYL (pointing timidly to the door)
I would rather go out that way....

THE FAIRY (growing suddenly angry again)
That's quite impossible; and it's a shocking habit!... (Pointing to the window) We'll go out this way.... Well?... What are you waiting for?... Get dressed at once.... (The CHILDREN *do as they are told and dress quickly*.) I'll help Mytyl....

TYLTYL
We have no shoes....

THE FAIRY
That doesn't matter. I will give you a little magic hat. Where are your father and mother?....

TYLTYL (pointing to the door on the right)
They're asleep in there....

THE FAIRY
And your grandpapa and grandmamma?...

TYLTYL
They're dead....

THE FAIRY
And your little brothers and sisters.... Have you any?...

TYLTYL
Oh, yes; three little brothers....

MYTYL
And four little sisters....

THE FAIRY
Where are they?...

TYLTYL
They are dead, too....

THE FAIRY
Would you like to see them again?...

TYLTYL
Oh, yes!... At once!... Show them to us!...

THE FAIRY
I haven't got them in my pocket.... But this is very lucky; you will see them when you go through the Land of Memory.... It's on the way to the Blue Bird, just on the left, past the third turning.... What were you doing when I knocked?...

TYLTYL
We were playing at eating cakes?...

THE FAIRY
Have you any cakes?... Where are they?...

TYLTYL
In the house of the rich children.... Come and look, it's so lovely. (He drags the FAIRY *to the window*.)

THE FAIRY (at the window)
But it's the others who are eating them!...

TYLTYL
Yes; but we can see them eat....

THE FAIRY
Aren't you cross with them?...

TYLTYL
What for?...

THE FAIRY
For eating all the cakes.... I think it's very wrong of them not to give you some....

TYLTYL
Not at all; they're rich.... I say, isn't it beautiful over there?...

THE FAIRY
It's no more beautiful there than here.

TYLTYL
Ugh!... It's darker here and smaller and there are no cakes....

THE FAIRY
It's exactly the same, only you can't see....

TYLTYL
Yes, I can; and I have very good eyes. I can see the time on the church clock and daddy can't...

THE FAIRY (suddenly angry)
I tell you that you can't see!... How do you see me?... What do I look like?... (An awkward silence from TYLTYL.) Well, answer me, will you? I want to know if you can see!... Am I pretty or ugly?... (The silence grows more and more uncomfortable.) Won't you answer?... Am I young or old?... Are my cheeks pink or yellow?... Perhaps you'll say I have a hump?...

TYLTYL (in a conciliatory tone)
No, no; It's not a big one....

THE FAIRY
Oh, yes, to look at you, any one would think it enormous.... Have I a hook nose and have I lost one of my eyes?...

TYLTYL
Oh, no, I don't say that.... Who put it out?...

THE FAIRY (growing more and more irritated).
But it's not out!... You wretched, impudent boy!... It's much finer than the other; it's bigger and brighter and blue as the sky.... And my hair, do you see that?... It's fair as the corn in the fields, it's like virgin gold!... And I've such heaps and heaps of it that it weighs my head down.... It escapes on every side.... Do you see it on my hands? (She holds out two lean wisps of grey hair.)

TYLTYL
Yes, I see a little....

THE FAIRY (indignantly)
A little!... Sheaves! Armfuls! Clusters! Waves of gold!... I know there are people who say that they don't see any; but you're not one of those wicked, blind people, I should hope?...

TYLTYL
Oh, no; I can see all that isn't hidden....

THE FAIRY
But you ought to see the rest with as little doubt!... Human beings are very odd!... Since the death of the fairies, they see nothing at all and they never suspect it.... Luckily, I always carry with me all that is

wanted to give new light to dimmed eyes.... What am I taking out of my bag?...

TYLTYL
Oh, what a dear little green hat!... What's that shining in the cockade?...

THE FAIRY
That's the big diamond that makes people see....

TYLTYL
Really?...

THE FAIRY
Yes; when you've got the hat on your head, you turn the diamond a little; from right to left, for instance, like this; do you see?... Then it presses a bump which nobody knows of and which opens your eyes....

TYLTYL
Doesn't it hurt?...

THE FAIRY
On the contrary, it's enchanted.... You at once see even the inside of things: the soul of bread, of wine, of pepper, for instance....

MYTYL
Can you see the soul of sugar, too?...

THE FAIRY (suddenly cross)
Of course you can!... I hate unnecessary questions.... The soul of sugar is no more interesting than the soul of pepper.... There, I give you all I have to help you in your search for the Blue Bird. I know that the flying carpet or the ring which makes its wearer invisible would be more useful to you.... But I have lost the key of the cupboard in which I locked them....

Oh, I was almost forgetting!... (Pointing to the diamond) When you hold it like this, do you see?... One little turn more and you behold the past.... Another little turn and you behold the future.... It's curious and practical and it's quite noiseless....

TYLTYL
Daddy will take it from me....

THE FAIRY
He won't see it; no one can see it as long as it's on your head.... Will you try it?... (She puts the little green hat on TYLTYL'S head.) Now, turn the diamond.... One turn and then....

(TYLTYL *has no sooner turned the diamond than a sudden and wonderful change comes over everything. The old* FAIRY *alters then and there into a princess of marvellous beauty; the flints of which the cottage walls are built light up, turn blue as sapphires, become transparent and gleam and sparkle like the most precious stones. The humble furniture takes life and becomes resplendent; the deal table assumes as grave and noble an air as a table made of marble; the face of the clock winks its eye and smiles genially, while the door that contains the pendulum opens and releases the Hours, which, holding one another by the hand and laughing merrily, begin to dance to the sound of delicious music*.)

TYLTYL (displaying a legitimate bewilderment and pointing to the Hours)
Who are all those pretty ladies?...

THE FAIRY
Don't be afraid; they are the hours of your life and they are glad to be free and visible for a moment....

TYLTYL

And why are the walls so bright?... Are they made of sugar or of precious stones?...

THE FAIRY

All stones are alike, all stones are precious; but man sees only a few of them....

(While they are speaking, the scene of enchantment continues and is completed. The souls of the Quartern-loaves, in the form of little men in crust-coloured tights, flurried and all powdered with flour, scramble out of the bread-pan and frisk round the table, where they are caught up by FIRE, *who, springing from the hearth in yellow and vermilion tights, writhes with laughter as he chases the loaves*.)

TYLTYL

Who are those ugly little men?...

THE FAIRY

Oh, they're nothing; they are merely the souls of the Quartern-loaves, who are taking advantage of the reign of truth to leave the pan in which they were too tightly packed....

TYLTYL

And the big red fellow, with the nasty smell?...

THE FAIRY

Hush!... Don't speak too loud; that's Fire.... He's dangerous. (This dialogue does not interrupt the enchantment. The DOG **and the** CAT, *lying rolled up at the foot of the cupboard, utter a loud and simultaneous cry and disappear down a trap; and in their places rise two persons, one of whom has the face of a bull-dog, the other that of a* *tom-cat. Forthwith, the little man with the bull-dog face, whom we will henceforward call the* DOG, *rushes upon* TYLTYL, *kisses him violently and overwhelms him with noisy and impetuous caresses; while the little man with the face of a tom-cat, whom we will simply call the* CAT, *combs his hair, washes his hands and strokes his whiskers before going up to* MYTYL.)

THE DOG (yelling, jumping about, knocking up against everything, unbearable)
My little god!... Good-morning, good-morning, my dear little god!... At last, at last we can talk!... I had so much to tell you!... Bark and wag my tail as I might, you never understood!... But now!... Good-morning, good-morning!... I love you!... Shall I do some of my tricks?... Shall I beg?... Would you like to see me walk on my front paws or dance on my hind-legs?...

TYLTYL (to the FAIRY)
Who is this gentleman with the dog's head?....

THE FAIRY
Don't you see? It's the soul of TYLO whom you have set free....

THE CAT (going up to MYTYL *and putting out his hand to her, with much ceremony and circumspection*)
Good-morning, Miss.... How well you look this morning!...

MYTYL
Good-morning, sir.... (To the FAIRY) Who is it?...

THE FAIRY
Why, don't you see? Its the soul of Tylette offering you his hand.... Kiss him....

THE DOG (hustling the CAT)
Me, too!... I've kissed the little god!... I've kissed the little girl!... I've kissed everybody!... Oh, grand!... What fun we shall have!... I'm going to frighten Tylette I Bow, wow, wow!...

THE CAT
Sir, I don't know you....

THE FAIRY (threatening the DOG *with her stick*)
Keep still, will you, or else you'll go back into silence until the end of time....

(Meanwhile, the enchantment has pursued its course: the spinning-wheel has begun to turn madly in its corner and to spin brilliant rays of light; the tap, in another corner, begins to sing in a very high voice and, turning into a luminous fountain, floods the sink with sheets of pearls and emeralds, through which darts the soul of WATER, *like a young girl, streaming, dishevelled and tearful, who immediately begins to fight with* FIRE.)

TYLTYL
And who is that wet lady?...

THE FAIRY
Don't be afraid. It's Water just come from the tap....

(The milk-jug upsets, falls from the table and smashes on the floor; and from the spilt milk there rises a tall, white, bashful figure who seems to be afraid of everything.)

TYLTYL
And the frightened lady in her nightgown?...

THE FAIRY
That's Milk; she has broken her jug....

(The sugar-loaf, at the foot of the cupboard, grows taller and wider and splits its paper wrapper, whence issues a mawkish and hypocritical being, dressed in a long coat half blue and half white, who goes up to MYTYL with a sanctimonious smile.)

MYTYL (greatly alarmed)
What does he want?...

THE FAIRY
Why, he is the soul of Sugar!...

MYTYL (reassured)
Has he any barley-sugar?...

THE FAIRY
His pockets are full of it and each of his fingers is a sugar-stick....

(The lamp falls from the table and, at the same moment, its flame springs up again and turns into a luminous maid of incomparable beauty. She is dressed in long transparent and dazzling veils and stands motionless in a sort of ecstasy.)

TYLTYL
It's the Queen!...

MYTYL
It's the Blessed Virgin!...

THE FAIRY
No, my children; it's Light....

(Meanwhile, the saucepans on the shelves spin round like tops; the linen-press throws open its folding-doors and unrolls a magnificent display of moon-coloured and sun-coloured stuffs, with which mingles a no less splendid array of rags and tatters that come down the ladder from the loft. But, suddenly, three loud knocks are heard on the door at the right.)

TYLTYL (alarmed)
That's daddy!... He's heard us!...

THE FAIRY
Turn the diamond!... From left to right!...

(TYLTYL *turns the diamond quickly*.)
Not so quick!... Heavens! It's too late!... You turned it too briskly; they will not have time to resume their places and we shall have a lot of annoyance....

(The FAIRY becomes an old woman again, the walls of the cottage lose their splendour. The Hours go back into the clock, the spinning-wheel stops, etc. But, in the general hurry and confusion, while FIRE *runs madly round the room, looking for the chimney, one of the loaves of bread, who has been unable to squeeze into the pan, bursts into sobs and utters roars of fright*.)

THE FAIRY
What's the matter?...

BREAD (in tears)
There's no room in the pan!...

THE FAIRY (stooping over the pan)
Yes, there is; yes, there is.... (Pushing the other loaves, which have

resumed their original places.) Come, quick, make room there....

(The knocking at the door is renewed.)

BREAD (utterly scared, vainly struggling to enter the pan)
I can't get in!... He'll eat me first!...

THE DOG (frisking round TYLTYL)
My little god!... I am still here!... I can still talk!... I can still kiss you!... Once more! Once more! Once more!...

THE FAIRY
What, you too?... Are you there still?...

THE DOG
What luck!... I was too late to return to silence; the trap closed too quickly....

THE CAT
So did mine.... What is going to happen?... Is there any danger?...

THE FAIRY
Well, I'm bound to tell you the truth: all those who accompany the two children will die at the end of the journey....

THE CAT (to the DOG)
Come, let us get back into the trap....

THE DOG
No, no!... I won't!... I want to go with the little god!... I want to talk to him all the time!...

THE CAT
Idiot!...

(More knocking at the door)

BREAD (shedding bitter tears)
I don't want to die at the end of the journey!... I want to get back at once into my pan!...

FIRE (who has done nothing but run madly round the room, hissing with anguish)
I can't find my chimney!...

WATER (vainly trying to get into the tap)
I can't get into the tap!...

SUGAR (hovering round his paper wrapper)
I've burst my packing-paper!...

MILK (lymphatically and bashfully)
Somebody's broken my little jug!...

THE FAIRY
Goodness me, what fools they are!... Fools and cowards too!... So you would rather go on living in your ugly boxes, in your traps and taps, than accompany the children in search of the bird?...

ALL (excepting the DOG *and* LIGHT)
Yes, yes! Now, at once!... My tap!... My pan!... My chimney!... My trap!...

THE FAIRY (to LIGHT, **who is dreamily gazing at the wreckage of her lamp**)

And you, Light, what do you say?

LIGHT
I will go with the children....

THE DOG (yelling with delight)
I too!... I too!...

THE FAIRY
That's right.... Besides, it's too late to go back; you have no choice now, you must all start with us.... But you, Fire, don't come near anybody; you, Dog, don't tease the Cat; and you, Water, hold yourself up and try not to run all over the place....

(A violent knocking is again heard at the door on the right.)

TYLTYL (listening)
There's daddy again!... He's getting up this time; I can hear him walking....

THE FAIRY
Let us go out by the window.... You shall all come to my house, where I will dress the Animals and the Things properly.... (To BREAD) You, Bread, take the cage in which to put the Blue Bird.... It will be in your charge.... Quick, quick, let us waste no time....

(The window suddenly lengthens downwards, like a door. They all go out; after which the window resumes its primitive shape and closes quite innocently. The room has become dark again and the two cots are steeped in shadow. The door on the right opens ajar and in the aperture appear the heads of DADDY *and* MUMMY TYL.)

DADDY TYL
It was nothing.... It's the cricket chirping....

MUMMY TYL
Can you see them?...

DADDY TYL
I can.... They are sleeping quite quietly....

MUMMY TYL
I can hear their breathing....

(The door closes again)

CURTAIN

ACT II

SCENE I.--At the FAIRY'S.

A magnificent entrance-hall in the palace of the FAIRY BERYLUNE. Columns of gleaming marble with gold and silver capitals, staircases, porticoes, balustrades, etc.

Enter from the back, on the right, sumptuously clad, the CAT, SUGAR and FIRE. *They come from a room which emits rays of light; it is the* FAIRY'S *wardrobe. The* CAT *has donned the classic costume of Puss-in-boots*; SUGAR, *a silk dress, half white and half pale-blue; and* FIRE *wears a number of many-coloured aigrettes and a long vermilion mantle lined with gold. They cross the whole length of the hall to the front of the stage, where the* CAT *draws them up under a portico on the right*.

THE CAT
This way, I know every inch of this palace. It was left to the Fairy Berylune by Bluebeard.... Let us make the most of our last minute of liberty, while the children and Light pay their visit to the Fairy's little daughter.... I have brought you here in order to discuss the position in which we are placed.... Are we all here?...

SUGAR
I see the Dog coming out of the Fairy's wardrobe....

FIRE
What on earth has he got on?...

THE CAT
He has put on the livery of one of the footmen of Cinderella's coach.... It was just the thing for him.... He has the soul of a flunkey.... But let us hide behind the balustrade.... It's strange how I mistrust him.... He had better not hear what I have to say to you....

SUGAR
It is too late.... He has discovered us.... Look, here is Water also coming out of the wardrobe.... Goodness me, how fine she is!...

(The DOG *and* WATER *join the first group*.)

THE DOG (frisking about)
There! There!... Aren't we fine I.... Just look at these laces and this embroidery!... It's real gold and no mistake!...

THE CAT (to WATER)
Is that Catskin's "colour-of-time" dress?... I seem to recognise it....

WATER
Yes, it's the one that suited me best....

FIRE (between his teeth)
She's not brought her umbrella....

WATER
What's that?...

FIRE
Nothing, nothing....

WATER
I thought you might be speaking of a great red I saw the other day....

THE CAT
Come, don't let as quarrel; we have more important things to do.... We are only waiting for Bread; where is he?

THE DOG
He was making an endless fuss about choosing his dress....

FIRE
Worth while, isn't it, for a fellow who looks a fool and carries an enormous stomach?...

THE DOG
At last, he decided in favour of a Turkish robe, adorned with gems, a scimitar and a turban....

THE CAT
There he is!... He has put on Bluebeard's finest dress...

Enter BREAD, *in the costume described above. The silk robe is crossed tightly over his huge stomach. In one hand he holds the hilt of a scimitar passed through his sash and in the other the cage intended for the Blue Bird.*

BREAD (waddling conceitedly)
Well?... What do you think of this?

THE DOG (frisking round the LOAF)

How nice he looks! What a fool he looks! How nice he looks! How nice he looks!...

THE CAT (to the LOAF)
Are the children dressed?...

BREAD
Yes, Master Tyltyl has put on Hop-o'-my-Thumb's blue jacket and red breeches; and Miss Mytyl has Gretel's frock and Cinderella's slippers.... But the great thing was the dressing of Light!...

THE CAT
Why?...

BREAD
The Fairy thought her so lovely that she did not want to dress her at all!... Thereupon I protested in the name of our dignity as essential and eminently respectable elements; and I ended by declaring that, under those conditions, I should refuse to be seen with her....

FIRE
They ought to have bought her a lampshade!...

THE CAT
And what answer did the Fairy make?...

THE LOAF
She hit me with her stick on my head and stomach....

THE CAT
And then?...

BREAD
I allowed myself to be convinced; but, at the last moment, Light decided on the moonbeam dress at the bottom of the chest with Catskin's treasures....

THE CAT
Come, stop chattering, time presses.... Our future is at stake.... You have heard--the Fairy has just said so--that the end of this journey will, at the same time, mark the end of our lives.... It is our business, therefore, to prolong it as much as possible and by every possible means.... But there is another thing: we must think of the fate of our race and the destiny of our children....

BREAD
Hear, hear!... The Cat is right!...

THE CAT
Listen to me!... All of us here present, Animals, Things and Elements, possess a soul which man does not yet know. That is why we retain a remnant of independence; but, if he finds the Blue Bird, he will know all, he will see all and we shall be completely at his mercy.... This is what I have just learned from my old friend, Night, who is also the guardian of the mysteries of Life.... It is to our interest, therefore, at all costs to prevent the finding of that bird, even if we have to go so far as to endanger the lives of the children themselves....

THE DOG (indignantly)
What's the fellow saying?... Just say that again, will you, to see if I heard right?...

BREAD
Order! Order!... It's not your turn to speak!... I'm in the chair at this meeting....

FIRE
Who made you chairman?...

WATER (to FIRE)
Hold your tongue!... What are you interfering with?...

FIRE
I shall interfere where I choose.... And I want none of your remarks....

SUGAR (concilatorily)
Excuse me.... Do not let us quarrel.... This is a serious moment.... We must, above all things, decide what measures to adopt....

BREAD
I quite agree with Sugar and the Cat....

THE DOG
This is ridiculous!... There is Man and that's all!... We have to obey him and do as he tells us!... That is the one and only fact!... I recognise no one but him!... Hurrah for Man!... Man for ever!... In life or death, all for Man!... Man is God!...

BREAD
I quite agree with the Dog.

THE CAT (to the DOG)
But at least give your reasons....

THE DOG
There are no reasons!... I love Man and that's enough!... If you do anything against him, I will throttle you first and I will go and tell him everything....

SUGAR (intervening sweetly)
Excuse me.... Let us not embitter the discussion.... From a certain point of view, you are both of you right.... There is something to be said on both sides....

BREAD
I quite agree with SUGAR!...

THE CAT
Are we not, all of us, Water, Fire you yourselves, Bread and the Dog, the victims of a nameless tyranny?... Do you remember the time when, before the coming of the despot, we wandered at liberty upon the face of the earth?... Fire and Water were the sole masters of the world; and see what they have come to!... As for us puny descendants of the great wild animals.... Look out!... Pretend to be doing nothing!... I see the Fairy and Light coming.... Light has taken sides with Man; she is our worst enemy.... Here they are....

Enter, on the right, the FAIRY, *in the shape of an old woman, and* LIGHT, *followed by* TYLTYL *and* MYTYL.

THE FAIRY
Well?... What is it?... What are you doing in that corner?... You look like conspirators.... It is time to start.... I have decided that Light shall be your leader.... You will obey her as you would me and I am giving her my wand.... The children will pay a visit to their late grandparents this evening.... You will remain behind; that is more discreet.... They will spend the evening in the bosom of their dead family.... Meanwhile, you will be getting ready all that is wanted for to-morrow's journey, which will be a long one.... Come, up, be off and every one to his post!...

THE CAT (hypocritically)
That is just what I was saying to them, madam.... I was encouraging them to

do their duty bravely and conscientiously; unfortunately, the Dog, who kept on interrupting me....

THE DOG
What's that?... Just wait a bit I...

(He is about to leap upon the CAT, **but** TYLTYL *foreseeing his intention, stops with a threatening gesture*.)

TYLTYL
Down, Tylo!... Take care; and, if ever I catch you again...

THE DOG
My little god, you don't know, it was he who...

TYLTYL (threatening him)
Be quiet!...

THE FAIRY
Come, that will do.... Let Bread hand the cage for this evening to Tyltyl.... It is just possible that the Blue Bird may be hidden In the Past, at the grandparents'.... In any case, it Is a chance which we must not neglect.... Well, Bread, the cage?

BREAD (solemnly)
One moment, if you please, Mrs. Fairy....
(Like an orator making a speech)
I call upon all of you to bear witness that this silver cage, which was entrusted to my care by....

THE FAIRY (interrupting him)
Enough!... No speeches!... We will go out this way and the children that....

TYLTYL (rather anxiously)
Are we to go all alone?...

MYTYL
I feel hungry!...

TYLTYL
I, too!...

THE FAIRY (to BREAD)
Open your Turkish robe and give them a slice of your good stomach....

(BREAD *opens his robe, draws his scimitar and cuts two slices out of his stomach and hands them to the* CHILDREN.)

SUGAR (approaching the CHILDREN)
Allow me at the same time to offer you a few sugar-sticks....
(He breaks off the five fingers of his left hand, one by one, and presents them to the CHILDREN.)

MYTYL
What is he doing?... He is breaking all his fingers!...

SUGAR (engagingly)
Taste them, they are capital... They're made of real barley-sugar....

MYTYL (tasting one of the fingers)
Oh, how good they are!... Have you many of them?...

SUGAR (modestly)
Yes; as many as I want....

MYTYL
Does that hurt you much, when you break them off?...

SUGAR
Not at all.... On the contrary, it's a great advantage; they grow again at once and so I always have new, clean fingers....

THE FAIRY
Come, children, don't eat too much sugar.... Don't forget that you are to have supper presently with your grandpapa and grandmamma....

TYLTYL
Are they here?...

THE FAIRY
You shall see them at once....

TYLTYL
How can we see them, when they are dead?...

THE FAIRY
How can they be dead, when they live in your memory?... Men do not know this secret, because they know so little; whereas you, thanks to the diamond, are about to see that the dead who are remembered live as happily as though they were not dead....

TYLTYL
Is Light coming with us?

THE FAIRY
No, it is more proper that this visit should be confined to the family.... I will wait near here, so as not to appear indiscreet.... They did not invite me....

TYLTYL
Which way are we to go?...

THE FAIRY
Over there.... You are on the threshold of the Land of Memory.... As soon as you have turned the diamond, you will see a big tree with a board on it, which will show you that you are there.... But don't forget that you are to be back, both of you, by a quarter to nine.... It is extremely important.... Now mind and be punctual, for all would be lost if you were late.... Good-bye for the present!...
(Calling the CAT, *the* DOG, LIGHT, *etc*.) This way.... And the little ones that way....

(She goes out to the right, with LIGHT, *the* ANIMALS, *etc., while the* CHILDREN *go out to the left*.)

CURTAIN

SCENE 2.--The Land of Memory.

A thick fog, from which stands out, on the right, close to the footlights, the trunk of a large oak, with a board nailed to it. A vague, milky, impenetrable light prevails. TYLTYL *and* MYTYL *are at the foot of the oak*.

TYLTYL
Here Is the tree!...

MYTYL
There's the board!...

TYLTYL
I can't read it.... Wait, I will climb up on this root.... That's it.... It says, "Land of Memory."

MYTYL
Is this where it begins?...

TYLTYL
Yes, there's an arrow....

MYTYL
Well, where are grandad and granny?...

TYLTYL
Behind the fog.... We shall see....

MYTYL
I can see nothing at all!... I can't see my feet or my hands....

(Whimpering) I'm cold!... I don't want to travel any more.... I want to go home....

TYLTYL
Come, don't keep on crying, just like Water.... You ought to be ashamed of yourself.... A great big little girl like you.... Look, the fog is lifting already.... We shall see what's behind it....

(The mist begins to move; It grows thinner and lighter, disperses, evaporates. Soon, in a more and more transparent light, appears, under a leafy vault, a cheerful little peasant's cottage, covered with creepers. The door and windows are open. There are bee-hives under a shed, flower-pots on the window-sills, a cage with a sleeping blackbird. Beside the door is a bench, on which an old peasant and his wife, TYLTYL'S grandfather and grandmother, are seated, both sound asleep.)

TYLTYL (suddenly recognising them)
It's grandad and granny!...

MYTYL (clapping her hands)
Yes! Yes!... So it is! So it is!...

TYLTYL (still a little distrustful)
Take care!... We don't know yet if they can stir.... Let's keep behind the tree....

(GRANNY TYL *opens her eyes, raises her head, stretches herself, gives a sigh and looks at* GAFFER TYL, *who also wakes slowly from his sleep*.)

GRANNY TYL
I have a notion that our grandchildren who are still alive are coming to see us today....

GAFFER TYL

They are certainly thinking of as, for I feel anyhow and I have pins and needles in my legs....

GRANNY TYL

I think they must be quite near, for I see tears of joy dancing before my eyes....

GAFFER TYL

No, no, they are a long way off.... I still feel weak....

GRANNY TYL

I tell you they are here; I am quite strong....

TYLTYL *and* MYTYL (rushing up from behind the oak)
Here we are!... Here we are!... Gaffer! Granny!... It's we!... It's we!...

GAFFER TYL

There!... You see?... What did I tell you?... I was sure they would come to-day....

GRANNY TYL

Tyltyl!... Mytyl!... It's you!... It's she!... (Trying to run to meet them) I can't run!... I've still got the rheumatics!...

GAFFER TYL (hobbling along as fast as he can)
No more can I.... That's because of my wooden leg, which I still wear instead of the one I broke when I fell off the big oak....

(The GRANDPARENTS *and the* CHILDREN *exchange frantic embraces*.)

GRANNY TYL
How tall and strong you've grown, Tyltyl!

GAFFER TYL (stroking MYTYL'S *hair*)
And Mytyl!... Just look at her.... What pretty hair, what pretty eyes!...

GRANNY TYL
Come and kiss me again!... Come on to my lap....

GAFFER TYL
And what about me?...

GRANNY TYL
No, no.... Come to me first.... How are Daddy and Mummy Tyl?...

TYLTYL
Quite well, granny.... They were asleep when we went out....

GRANNY TYL (gazing at them and covering them with caresses)
Lord, how pretty they are and how nice and clean!... Was it mummy who washed you?... And there are no holes in your stockings!... I used to darn them once, you know.... Why don't you come to see us oftener?... It makes us so happy!... It is months and months now that you've forgotten us and that we have seen nobody....

TYLTYL
We couldn't, granny; and to-day its only because of the Fairy....

GRANNY TYL
We are always here, waiting for a visit from those who are alive.... They come so seldom!... The last time you were here, let me see, when was it?... It was on All-hallows, when the church-bells were ringing....

TYLTYL
All-hallows?... We didn't go out that day, for we both had very bad colds....

GRANNY TYL
No; but you thought of us....

TYLTYL
Yes....

GRANNY TYL
Well, every time you think of us, we wake up and see you again....

TYLTYL
What, is it enough to...

GRANNY TYL
But come, you know that....

TYLTYL
No, I didn't know....

GRANNY TYL (to GAFFER TYL)
It's astonishing, up there.... They don't know yet.... Do they never learn anything?...

GAFFER TYL
It's as in our own time.... The Living are so stupid when they speak of the Others....

TYLTYL
Do you sleep all the time?...

GAFFER TYL
Yes, we get plenty of sleep, while waiting for a thought of the Living to come and wake us.... Ah, it is good to sleep when life is done.... But it is pleasant also to wake up from time to time....

TYLTYL
So you are not really dead?...

GAFFER TYL
What do you say?... What is he saying?... Now he's using words we don't understand.... Is it a new word, a new invention?...

TYLTYL
The word "dead"?...

GAFFER TYL
Yes, that was the word.... What does it mean?...

TYLTYL
Why, it means that one's no longer alive....

GAFFER TYL
How silly they are, up there!...

TYLTYL
Is it nice here?...

GAFFER TYL
Oh, yes; not bad, not bad; and, if one could just have a smoke....

TYLTYL
Aren't you allowed to smoke?...

GAFFER TYL
Yes, it's allowed; but I've broken my pipe....

GRANNY TYL
Yes, yes, all would be well, if only you would come and see us oftener.... Do you remember, Tyltyl?... The last time I baked you a lovely apple-tart.... You ate such a lot of it that you made yourself ill....

TYLTYL
But I haven't eaten any apple-tart since last year.... There were no apples this year....

GRANNY TYL
Don't talk nonsense.... Here, we have them always....

TYLTYL
That's different....

GRANNY TYL
What? That's different?... Why, nothing's different when we're able to kiss each other....

TYLTYL (looking first at his GRANDMOTHER *and then at his* GRANDFATHER)
You haven't changed, grandad, not a bit, not a bit.... And granny hasn't changed a bit either.... But you're better-looking....

GAFFER TYL
Well, we feel all right.... We have stopped growing older.... But you, how tall you're growing!... Yes, you're shooting up finely.... Look, over there, on the door, is the mark of the last time.... That was on All-hallows.... Now then, stand up straight.... (TYLTYL *stands up against the door.*) Four fingers taller!... That's immense!... (MYTYL

also stands up against the door.) And Mytyl, four and a half!...
Aha, ill weeds grow apace!... How they've grown, oh, how they've grown!...

TYLTYL (looking around him with delight)
Nothing is changed, everything is in its old place!... Only everything is prettier!... There is the clock with the big hand which I broke the point off....

GAFFER TYL
And here is the soup-tureen you chipped a corner off....

TYLTYL
And here is the hole which I made in the door, the day I found the gimlet....

GAFFER TYL
Yes, you've done some damage in your time!... And here is the plum-tree in which you were so fond of climbing, when I wasn't looking.... It still has its fine red plums....

TYLTYL
But they are finer than ever!...

MYTYL
And here is the old blackbird!... Does he still sing?...

(The blackbird wakes and begins to sing at the top of his voice.)

GRANNY TYL
You see.... As soon as one thinks of him....

TYLTYL (observing with amazement that the blackbird is quite blue)
But he's blue!... Why, that's the bird, the Blue Bird which I am to take

back to the Fairy.... And you never told us that you had him here!... Oh, he's blue, blue, blue as a blue glass marble!... (Entreatingly) Grandad, granny, will you give him to me?...

GAFFER TYL
Yes, perhaps, perhaps.... What do you think, granny?...

GRANNY TYL
Certainly, certainly.... What use is he to us?... He does nothing but sleep.... We never hear him sing....

TYLTYL
I will put him in my cage.... I say, where is my cage?... Oh, I know, I left it behind the big tree.... (He runs to the tree, fetches the cage and puts the blackbird into it.) So, really, you've really given him to me?... How pleased the Fairy will be!... And Light too!...

GAFFER TYL
Mind you, I won't answer for the bird.... I'm afraid that he will never get used again to the restless life up there and that he'll come back here by the first wind that blows this way.... However, we shall see.... Leave him there, for the present, and come and look at the cow....

TYLTYL (noticing the hives)
And how are the bees getting on?

GAFFER TYL
Oh, pretty well.... They are no longer alive, as you call it up there; but they work hard....

TYLTYL (going up to the hives)
Oh, yes!... I can smell the honey!... How heavy the hives must be!... All the flowers are so beautiful!... And my little dead sisters, are they here

too?...

MYTYL
And where are my three little brothers who were buried?...

(At these words, seven little CHILDREN, *of different sizes, like a set of Pan's pipes, come out of the cottage, one by one*.)

GRANNY TYL
Here they are, here they are!... As soon as you think of them, as soon as you speak of them, they are there, the darlings!...

(TYLTYL *and* MYTYL *run to meet the* CHILDREN. *They hustle and hug one another and dance and whirl about and utter screams of joy*.)

TYLTYL
Hullo, Pierrot!... (They clutch each other by the hair.) Ah, so we're going to fight again, as in the old days.... And Robert!... I say, Jean, what's become of your top?... Madeleine and Pierette and Pauline!... And here's Riquette!...

MYTYL
Oh, Riquette, Riquette!... She's still crawling on all fours!...

GRANNY TYL
Yes, she has stopped growing.

TYLTYL (noticing the little DOG *yelping around them*)
There's Kiki, whose tail I cut off with Pauline's scissors.... He hasn't changed either....

GAFFER TYL (sententiously)
No, nothing changes here....

TYLTYL
And Pauline still has a pimple on her nose....

GRANNY TYL
Yes, it won't go away; there's nothing to be done for it....

TYLTYL
Oh, how well they look, how fat and glossy they are!... What jolly cheeks they have!... They look well fed....

GRANNY TYL
They have been much better since they ceased living.... There's nothing more to fear, nobody is ever ill, one has no anxiety....

(The clock inside the cottage strikes eight.)

GRANNY TYL (amazed)
What's that?...

GAFFER TYL
I don't know, I'm sure.... It must be the clock....

GRANNY TYL
It can't be.... It never strikes....

GAFFER TYL
Because we no longer think of the time.... Was any one thinking of the time?...

TYLTYL
Yes, I was.... What is the time?...

GAFFER TYL
I'm sure I can't tell.... I've forgotten how.... It struck eight times, so I suppose it's what they call eight o'clock up there....

TYLTYL
Light expects me at a quarter to nine.... It's because of the Fairy.... It's extremely important.... I'm off!...

GRANNY TYL
Don't leave us like that, just as supper's ready!... Quick, quick, let's lay the table outside.... I've got some capital cabbage-soup and a beautiful plum-tart....

(They get out the table, dishes, plates, etc., and lay for supper outside the door, all helping.)

TYLTYL
Well, as I've got the Blue Bird.... And then it's so long since I tasted cabbage-soup.... Ever since I've been, travelling.... They don't have it at the hotels....

GRANNY TYL
There!... That didn't take long!... Sit down, children.... Don't let us lose time, if you're in a hurry....

(They have lit the lamp and served the soup. The GRANDPARENTS *and the* CHILDREN *sit down round the table, jostling and elbowing one another and laughing and screaming with pleasure*.)

TYLTYL (eating like a glutton)
How good it is!... Oh, how good it is!...I want some more! More!...

(He brandishes his wooden spoon and noisily hits his plate with it.)

GAFFER TYL
Come, come, a little more quiet.... You're just as ill-behaved as ever; and you'll break your plate....

TYLTYL (half-raising himself on his stool)
I want more, more!... (He seizes the tureen, drags it toward him and upsets it and the soup, which trickles over the table and down over their knees and scalds them. Yells and screams of pain.)

GRANNY TYL
There!... I told you so!...

GAFFER TYL (giving TYLTYL a loud box on the ear)
That's one for you!...

TYLTYL (staggered for a moment, next puts his hand to his cheek with an expression of rapture)
Oh, that's just like the slaps you used to give me when you were alive?... Grandad, how nice it was and how good it makes one feel!... I must give you a kiss!...

GAFFER TYL
Very well; there's more where that came from, if you like them....

(The clock strikes half-past eight)

TYLTYL (starting up)
Half-past eight!... (He flings down his spoon.) Mytyl, we've only just got time!...

GRANNY TYL
Oh, I say!... Just a few minutes more!... Your house isn't on fire!... We see you so seldom....

TYLTYL
No, we can't possibly.... Light is so kind.... And I promised her.... Come, Mytyl, come!...

GAFFER TYL
Goodness gracious, how tiresome the Living are with all their business and excitement!...

TYLTYL (taking his cage and hurriedly kissing everybody all round)
Good-bye, grandad.... Good-bye, granny.... Good-bye, brothers and sisters, Pierrot, Robert, Pauline, Madeleine, Riquette and you, too, Kiki.... I feel we mustn't stay.... Don't cry, granny; we will come back often....

GRANNY TYL
Come back every day!...

TYLTYL
Yes, yes; we will come back as often as we can....

GRANNY TYL
It's our only pleasure and it's such a treat for us when your thoughts visit us!...

GAFFER TYL
We have no other amusements....

TYLTYL
Quick, quick!... My cage!... My bird!...

GAFFER TYL (handing him the cage)
Here they are!... You know, I don't warrant him; and if he's not the right colour...

TYLTYL
Good-bye! Good-bye!...

THE BROTHERS AND SISTERS TYL
Good-bye, Tyltyl! Good-bye, Mytyl!... Remember the barley-sugar!... Good-bye!... Come again!... Come again!...

(They all wave their handkerchiefs while TYLTYL *and* MYTYL slowly move away. But already, during the last sentences, the fog of the beginning of the scene has been gradually re-forming, so that, at the end, all has disappeared in the mist and, at the fall of the curtain, TYLTYL and MYTYL *are again alone visible under the big oak*.)

TYLTYL
It's this way, Mytyl....

MYTYL
Where is Light?...

TYLTYL
I don't know.... (Looking at the bird in the cage.) But the bird is no longer blue!... He has turned black!...

MYTYL
Give me your hand, little brother.... I feel so frightened and so cold....

ACT III.

SCENE 1.--The Palace of NIGHT.

A large and wonderful hall of an austere, rigid, metallic and sepulchral magnificence, giving the impression of a Greek temple with columns, architraves, flagstones and ornaments of black marble, gold and ebony. The hall is trapezium-shaped. Basalt steps, occupying almost the entire width, divide it into three successive stages, which rise gradually toward the back. On the right and left, between the columns, are doors of sombre bronze. At the back, a monumental door of brass. The palace is lit only by a vague light that seems to emanate mainly from the brilliancy of the marble and the ebony. At the rise of the curtain, NIGHT, *in the form of a very old woman, clad in long, black garments, is seated on the steps of the second stage between two children, of whom one, almost naked, like Cupid, is smiling in a deep sleep, while the other is standing up, motionless and veiled from head to foot*.

Enter from the right, in the foreground, the CAT

NIGHT
Who goes there?

THE CAT (sinking heavily upon the marble steps)
It is I, Mother Night.... I am worn out....

NIGHT
What's the matter, child?... You look pale and thin and you are splashed with mud to your very whiskers.... Have you been fighting on the tiles again, in the snow and rain?...

THE CAT
It has nothing to do with the tiles!... It's our secret that's at stake!... It's the beginning of the end!... I have managed to escape for a moment to warn you; but I greatly fear that there is nothing to be done....

NIGHT
Why?... What has happened?...

THE CAT
I have told you of little Tyltyl, the woodcutter's son, and of the magic diamond.... Well, he is coming here to demand the Blue Bird of you....

NIGHT
He hasn't got it yet.....

THE CAT
He will have it soon, unless we perform some miracle.... This is how the matter stands: Light, who is guiding him and betraying us all, for she has placed herself entirely on Man's side, Light has learned that the Blue Bird, the real one, the only one that can live in the light of day, is hidden here, among the blue birds of the dreams that live on the rays of the moon and die as soon as they set eyes on the sun.... She knows that she is forbidden to cross the threshold of your palace, but she is sending the children; and, as you cannot prevent Man from opening the doors of your secrets, I do not know how all this will end.... In any case, if,

unfortunately, they should lay their hands on the real Blue Bird, there would be nothing for us but to disappear....

NIGHT
Oh dear, oh dear!.... What times we live in!... I never have a moment's peace.... I cannot understand Man, these last few years.... What is he aiming at?... Must he absolutely know everything?... Already he has captured a third of my Mysteries, all my Terrors are afraid and dare not leave the house, my Ghosts have taken flight, the greater part of my Sicknesses are ill....

THE CAT
I know, Mother Night, I know, the times are hard and we are almost alone in our struggle against Man.... But I hear them coming.... I see only one way: as they are children, we must give them such a fright that they will not dare to persist or to open the great door at the back, behind which they would find the Birds of the Moon.... The secrets of the other caverns will be enough to distract their attention and terrify them....

NIGHT (listening to a sound outside)
What do I hear?... Are there many of them?...

THE CAT
It is nothing; it is our friends, Bread and Sugar; Water is not very well and Fire could not come, because he is related to Light.... The Dog is the only one who is not on our side; but it is never possible to keep him away....

(Enter timidly, on the right, in the foreground, TYLTYL, MYTYL, BREAD, SUGAR and the DOG.)

THE CAT (rushing up to TYLTYL)
This way, little master, this way.... I have told Night, who is delighted

to see you.... You must forgive her, she is a little indisposed; that is why she was not able to come to meet you....

TYLTYL
Good-day, Mrs. Night....

NIGHT (in an offended voice)
Good-day?... I am not used to that.... You might say, Good-night, or, at least. Good-evening....

TYLTYL (mortified)
I beg your pardon, ma'am....I did not know....(Pointing to the two CHILDREN.) Are those your two little boys?... They are very nice....

NIGHT
This is Sleep....

TYLTYL
Why is he so fat?...

NIGHT
That is because he sleeps well....

TYLTYL
And the other, hiding himself?... Why does he veil his face?...Is he ill?... What is his name?...

NIGHT
That is Sleep's sister.... It is better not to mention her name....

TYLTYL
Why?...

NIGHT
Because her name is not pleasant to hear.... But let us talk of something else.... The Cat tells me that you have come here to look for the Blue Bird....

TYLTYL
Yes, ma'am, if you will allow me.... Will you tell me where he is?...

NIGHT
I don't know, dear.... All I can say is that he is not here.... I have never seen him....

TYLTYL
Yes, yes.... Light told me that he was here; and Light knows what she is saying.... Will you hand me your keys?...

NIGHT
But you must understand, dear, that I cannot give my keys like that to the first comer.... I have the keeping of all Nature's secrets and I am absolutely forbidden to deliver them to anybody, especially to a child....

TYLTYL
You have no right to refuse them to Man when he asks you for them....I know that....

NIGHT
Who told you?...

TYLTYL
Light....

NIGHT
Light again! Always Light!... How dare she interfere, how dare she?...

THE DOG
Shall I take them from her by force, my little god?...

TYLTYL
Hold your tongue, keep quiet and try to behave.... (To NIGHT) Come, madam, give me your keys, please....

NIGHT
Have you the sign, at least?... Where is it?...

TYLTYL (touching his hat)
Behold the Diamond!...

NIGHT (resigning herself to the inevitable)
Well, then... Here is the key that opens all the doors of the hall.... Look to yourself if you meet with a misfortune.... I will not be responsible....

BREAD (very anxiously)
Is it dangerous?...

NIGHT
Dangerous?... I will go so far as to say that I myself do not know what I shall do when certain of those bronze doors open upon the abyss.... All around the hall, in each of those basalt caves, are all the evils, all the plagues, all the sicknesses, all the terrors, all the catastrophes, all the mysteries that have afflicted life since the beginning of the world.... I have had trouble enough to Imprison them there with the aid of Destiny; and it is not without difficulty, I assure you, that I keep some little order among those undisciplined characters.... You have seen what happens when one of them escapes and shows itself on earth....

BREAD
My great age, my experience and my devotion make me the natural protector

of these two children; therefore, Mrs. Night, permit me to ask you a question....

NIGHT
Certainly....

BREAD
In case of danger, which is the way of escape?...

NIGHT
There is no way of escape.

TYLTYL (taking the key and climbing the first steps)
Let us begin here.... What is behind this bronze door?...

NIGHT
I think it is the Ghosts.... It is long since I opened the door and since they came out....

TYLTYL (placing the key in the lock)
I will see.... (To BREAD) Have you the cage for the Blue Bird?...

BREAD (with chattering teeth)
I'm not frightened, but don't you think it would be better not to open the door, but to peep through the keyhole?...

TYLTYL
I don't want your advice....

MYTYL (suddenly beginning to cry)
I am frightened!... Where is Sugar?... I want to go home!...

SUGAR (eagerly, obsequiously)
Here I am, miss, here I am.... Don't cry, I will break off one of my fingers so that you may have a sugar-stick....

TYLTYL
Enough of this!...

(He turns the key and cautiously opens the door. Forthwith, five or six GHOSTS *of strange and different forms escape and disperse on every side*. MYTYL *gives a scream of fright*, BREAD, *terrified, throws away the cage and goes and hides at the back of the hall, while* NIGHT, *running after the* GHOSTS, *cries out to* TYLTYL.)

NIGHT
Quick! Quick!... Shut the door!... They will all escape and we should never be able to catch them again!... They have felt bored in there, ever since Man ceased to take them seriously....
(She runs after the GHOSTS *and endeavours, with the aid of a whip formed of snakes, to drive them back to the door of their prison*.)
Help me!... Here!... Here!...

TYLTYL (to the DOG)
Help her, Tylo, at them!...

THE DOG (leaping up and barking)
Yes, yes, yes!...

TYLTYL
And Bread, where's Bread?...

BREAD (at the back of the hall)
Here.... I am near the door to prevent them from going out....

(One of the GHOSTS *moves in that direction and he rushes away at full speed, uttering yells of terror*.)

NIGHT (to three GHOSTS *whom she has seized by the neck*)
This way, you!... (To TYLTYL) Open the door a little.... (She pushes the GHOSTS *into the cave*.) There, that's it....
(The DOG *brings up two more*.) And these two.... Come, quick, in with you!... You know you're only allowed out on All-hallows....

(She closes the door.)

TYLTYL (going to another door)
What's behind this one?....

NIGHT
What is the good?...I have already told you the Blue Bird has never been here.... However, as you please.... Open the doors if you like.... It's the Sicknesses....

TYLTYL (with the key in the lock.)
Must I be careful in opening?...

NIGHT
No, it is not worth while.... They are very quiet, the poor little things.... They are not happy.... Man, for some time, has been waging such a determined war upon them!... Especially since the discovery of the microbes.... Open, you will see....

(TYLTYL *opens the door quite wide. Nothing appears*.)

TYLTYL
Don't they come out?

NIGHT
I told you they are almost all poorly and very much discouraged....
The doctors are so unkind to them.... Go in for a moment and see for
yourself....

(TYLTYL *enters the cavern and comes out again immediately*.)

TYLTYL
The Blue Bird is not there.... They look very ill, those Sicknesses of
yours.... They did not even lift their heads.... (One little Sickness in
slippers, a dressing-gown and a cotton nightcap escapes from the cavern
and begins to frisk about the hall.) Look!... There's a little one
escaping.... Which one is it?...

NIGHT
It's nothing, one of the smallest; it's Cold-in-the-Head.... It is one
of those which are least persecuted and which enjoy the best health....
(Calling to COLD-IN-THE-HEAD) Come here, dear....It's too soon yet;
you must wait for the winter.... (COLD-IN-THE-HEAD, *sneezing, coughing
and blowing its nose, returns to the cavern and* TYLTYL *shuts the
door*.)

TYLTYL (going to the next door)
Let us look at this one..... What is in here?...

NIGHT
Take care!... It is the Wars.... They are more terrible and powerful
than ever.... Heaven knows what would happen if one of them escaped!...
Fortunately, they are rather heavy and slow-moving.... But we must stand
ready to push back the door, all of us together, while you take a rapid
glance into the cavern....

(TYLTYL, *with a thousand precautions, opens the door ajar so that there is only a little gap to which he can put his eye. He at once doubles his back against the door, shouting*.)

TYLTYL
Quick! Quick!... Push with all your might!... They have seen me!... They are all coming!... They are breaking down the door!...

NIGHT
Come, all together!... Push hard!... Bread, what are you doing?... Push, all of you!... How strong they are!... Ah, that's it!... They are giving way!... It was high time!... Did you see them?...

TYLTYL
Yes, yes!... They are huge and awful!... I don't think that they have the Blue Bird....

NIGHT
You may be sure they haven't.... If they had, they would eat him at once.... Well, have you had enough of it?... You see there is nothing to be done....

TYLTYL
I must see everything.... Light said so....

NIGHT
Light said so!... It's an easy thing to say when one's afraid and stays at home....

TYLTYL
Let us go to the next.... What is in here?...

NIGHT
This is where I lock up the Shades and the Terrors....

TYLTYL
Can I open the door?...

NIGHT
Certainly.... They are pretty quiet; they are like the Sicknesses....

TYLTYL (half-opening the door, with a certain mistrustfulness, and taking a look into the cavern)
Are they not there?...

NIGHT (looking into the cavern in her turn)
Well, Shades, what are you doing?... Come out for a moment and stretch your legs; it will do you good.... And the Terrors also.... There is nothing to be afraid of.... (A few SHADES *and a few* TERRORS, *in the shape of women, shrouded, the former in black veils and the latter in greenish veils, piteously venture to take a few steps outside the cavern; and then, upon a movement of* TYLTYL'S, *hastily run back again*.)
Come, don't be afraid.... It's only a child; he won't hurt you....
(To TYLTYL) They have become extremely timid, except the great ones, those whom you see at the back....

TYLTYL (looking into the depths of the cave)
Oh, how terrifying they are!...

NIGHT
They are chained up.... They are the only ones that are not afraid of Man.... But shut the door, lest they should grow angry....

TYLTYL (going to the next door)
I say!... This is a darker one.... What is here?

NIGHT
There are several Mysteries behind this one.... If you are absolutely bent upon it, you may open it too.... But don't go in.... Be very cautious and let us get ready to push back the door, as we did with the Wars....

TYLTYL (half-opening the door; with unparalleled precautions and passing his head fearsomely through the aperture)
Oh!... How cold!... My eyes are smarting!... Shut it quickly!... Push, oh, push! They are pushing against us!... (NIGHT, *the* DOG, *the* CAT *and* SUGAR *push back the door*.) Oh, I saw!...

NIGHT
What?...

TYLTYL (upset)
I don't know, it was awful!... They were all seated like monsters without eyes.... Who was the giant who tried to seize me?...

NIGHT
It was probably Silence; he has charge of this door.... It appears to have been alarming?... You are quite pale still and trembling all over....

TYLTYL
Yes, I would never have believed.... I had never seen.... And my hands are frozen....

NIGHT
It will be worse presently if you go on....

TYLTYL (going to the next door)
And this one?... Is this terrible also?...

NIGHT
No; there is a little of everything here.... It is where I keep the unemployed Stars, my personal Perfumes, a few Glimmers that belong to me, such as Will-o'-the-Wisps, Glow-worms and Fireflies, also the Dew, the Song of the Nightingales and so on....

TYLTYL
Just so, the Stars, the Song of the Nightingales.... This must be the door....

NIGHT
Open it, if you like; there Is nothing very bad inside....

(TYLTYL *throws the door wide open. The* STARS, *in the shape of beautiful young girls veiled in many-coloured radiancy, escape from their prison, disperse over the hall and form graceful groups on the steps and around the columns, bathed in a sort of luminous penumbra. The* PERFUMES
OF THE NIGHT, *who are almost invisible, the* WILL-O'-THE-WISPS, the FIREFLIES *and the transparent* DEW *join them, while the* SONG OF THE NIGHTINGALES *streams from the cavern and floods the Palace of* NIGHT.)

MYTYL (clapping her hands with delight)
Oh, what pretty ladies!...

TYLTYL
And how well they dance!...

MYTYL
And how sweet they smell!...

TYLTYL
And how beautifully they sing!...

MYTYL
What are those, whom one can hardly see?...

NIGHT
Those are the Perfumes of my Shadow.

TYLTYL
And those others, over there, in spun glass?...

NIGHT
They are the Dew of the plains and forests.... But enough!... They would never have done.... It is the devil's own business to get them back, once they begin to dance.... (Clapping her hands together.) Now then, Stars, quick!... This is not the time for dancing.... The sky is overcast and heavily clouded.... Come, quick, in with you, or I will go and fetch a ray of sunlight!... (The STARS, PERFUMES, *etc., take to flight in dismay and rush back into the cavern; and the door is closed upon them. At*
the same time, the song of the NIGHTINGALE *ceases*.)

TYLTYL (going to the door at the back)
Here is the great middle door....

NIGHT (gravely)
Do not open that one...

TYLTYL
Why not?....

NIGHT
Because it's not allowed....

TYLTYL
Then it's here that the Blue Bird is hidden; Light told me so....

NIGHT (maternally)
Listen to me, child ... I have been kind and indulgent ... I have done for you what I have never done for any one before ... I have given up all my secrets to you.... I like you, I feel pity for your youth and innocence and I am speaking to you as a mother.... Listen to me, my child, and believe me; relinquish your quest, go no further, do not tempt fate, do not open that door....

TYLTYL (a little shaken)
But why?...

NIGHT
Because I do not wish you to be lost.... Because not one of those, do you hear, not one of those who have opened it, were it but by a hair's breadth, has ever returned alive to the light of day.... Because every awful thing imaginable, because all the terrors, all the horrors of which men speak on earth are as nothing compared with the most harmless of those which assail a man from the moment when his eye lights upon the first threats of the abyss to which no one dares give a name.... So much so that I myself, if you are bent, in spite of everything, upon touching that door, will ask you to wait until I have sought safety in my windowless tower... Now it is for you to know, for you to reflect....

(MYTYL, *all in tears, utters cries of inarticulate terror and tries to drag* TYLTYL *away*.)

BREAD (with chattering teeth)
Don't do it, master dear!... (Flinging himself on his knees) Take pity on us!... I implore you on my knees.... You see that Night is right....

THE CAT
You are sacrificing the lives of all of us....

TYLTYL
I must open the door....

MYTYL (stamping her feet, amid her sobs)
I won't!... I sha'n't!...

TYLTYL
Sugar and Bread, take Mytyl by the hand and run away with her.... I am going to open the door....

NIGHT
Run for your lives!... Come quickly!... It is time!... (She flees.)

BREAD (fleeing wildly)
At least wait till we are at the end of the hall!...

THE CAT (also fleeing)
Wait! Wait!...

(They hide behind the columns at the other end of the hall. TYLTYL remains alone with the DOG by the monumental door.)

THE DOG (panting and hiccoughing with suppressed fright)
I shall stay, I shall stay!... I'm not afraid!... I shall stay!... I shall stay with my little god!... I shall stay!... I shall stay!...

TYLTYL (patting the DOG)
That's right, Tylo, that's right!... Kiss me.... You and I are two.... And now, steady!...

(He places the key in the lock. A cry of alarm comes from the other end of the hall, where the runaways have taken refuge. The key has hardly touched the door before its tall and wide leaves open in the middle, glide apart and disappear on either side in the thickness of the walls, suddenly revealing the most unexpected of gardens, unreal, infinite and ineffable, a dream-garden bathed in nocturnal light, where, among stars and planets, illumining all that they touch, flying ceaselessly from jewel to jewel and from moonbeam to moonbeam, fairy-like blue birds hover perpetually and harmoniously down to the confines of the horizon, birds innumerable to the point of appearing to be the breath, the azured atmosphere, the very substance of the wonderful garden.)

TYLTYL (dazzled, bewildered, standing in the light of the garden)
Oh!... Heaven!... (Turning to those who have fled) Come quickly!... They are here!... It's they, it's they, it's they!... We have them at last!... Thousands of blue birds!... Millions!.... Thousands of millions!... There will be too many!... Come, Mytyl!... Come, Tylo!... Come, all!... Help me!... (Darting in among the birds.) You can catch them by handfuls!... They are not shy!... They are not afraid of us!.... Here! Here!.... (MYTYL **and the others run up. They all enter the dazzling garden, except** NIGHT **and the** CAT.) You see!... There are too many of them!... They fly into my hands!... Look, they are eating the moonbeams!... Mytyl, where are you?.... There are so many blue wings, so many feathers falling that one cannot see anything for them!.... Don't bite them, Tylo!.... Don't hurt them!.... Take them very gently!....

MYTYL (covered with blue birds)
I have caught seven already!.... Oh, how they flap their wings!.... I can't hold them!....

TYLTYL
Nor can I!.... I have too many of them!... They're escaping!.... They're coming back!.... Tylo has some, too!.... They will drag us with them!.... They will take us up to the sky!.... Quick, let us go out this way!.... Light is waiting for us!.... How pleased she will be!.... This way, this way!....

(They escape from the garden, with their hands full of struggling birds, and, crossing the whole hall amid the mad whirl of the azure wings, go out on the right, where they first entered, followed by BREAD *and* SUGAR, *who have caught no birds*. NIGHT *and the* CAT, *left alone, return to the back of the stage and look anxiously into the garden*.)

NIGHT
Haven't they got him?...

THE CAT
No.... I see him there, on that moonbeam.... They could not reach him, he kept too high....

(The CURTAIN *falls. Immediately after, before the dropped curtain*, ENTER, *at the same time, on the left*, LIGHT *and on the right*, TYLTYL, MYTYL *and the* DOG, *who run up all covered by the birds which they have captured. But already the birds appear lifeless and, with hanging heads and drooping wings, are nothing more in their hands than inert remains*.)

LIGHT
Well, have you caught him?...

TYLTYL
Yes, yes!...As many as we wanted!... There are thousands of them!... Here they are!... Do you see them?... (Looking at the birds, which he holds out to LIGHT, **and perceiving that they are dead**) Why, they are dead!... What have they done to them?... Yours too, Mytyl?... Tylo's also?... (Angrily flinging down the dead bodies of the birds) Oh, this is too bad?... Who killed them?... I am too unhappy!...

(He hides his head in his arms and his whole frame is shaken with sobs.)

LIGHT (pressing him maternally in her arms)
Do not cry, my child.... You did not catch the one that is able to live in broad daylight.... He has gone elsewhere.... We shall find him again....

THE DOG (looking at the dead birds))
Are they good to eat?....

(They all go out on the left.)

SCENE 2.--The Forest.

A forest. It is night. The moon is shining. Old trees of various kinds, notably an OAK, *a* BEECH, *an* ELM, *a* POPLAR, *a* FIR-TREE, *a* CYPRESS, *a* LIME-TREE, *a* CHESTNUT-TREE, *etc*.

ENTER *the* CAT.

THE CAT (bowing to the trees in turn)
To all the trees here present, greeting!....

THE TREES (murmuring in their leaves)
Greeting!....

THE CAT
This is a great day, a day of days!.... Our enemy is coming to set free your energies and to deliver himself into your hands..... It is Tyltyl, the son of the wood-cutter, who has done you so much harm.... He is seeking the Blue Bird, whom you have kept hidden from Man since the beginning of the world and who alone knows our secret.... (A murmuring in the leaves.) What do you say?... Ah, it's the Poplar!... Yes, he possesses a diamond which has the virtue of setting free our spirits for a moment; he can compel us to hand over the Blue Bird and thenceforth we shall be definitely at Man's mercy.... (A murmuring in the leaves.) Who is speaking?... Ah, the Oak!... How are you?... (A murmuring in the leaves of the OAK.) Still got your cold?... Does the Liquorice no longer look after you?... Can't you throw off your rheumatism?... Believe me, that's because of the moss; you put too much of it on your feet.... Is the Blue Bird still with you?... (A murmuring in the leaves of the OAK.) I beg your pardon?... Yes, there is no room for hesitation; we must take the opportunity; he must he done away with.... (A murmuring in the

leaves.) I didn't quite catch.... Oh, yes, he is with his little sister; she must die, too.... (A murmuring in the leaves.) Yes, they have the Dog with them; there is no keeping him away.... (A murmuring in the leaves.) What did you say?... Bribe him?... Impossible.... I have tried everything.... (A murmuring in the leaves.) Ah, is that you, Fir-Tree?... Yes, get four planks ready.... Yes, there are Fire, Sugar, Water and Bread besides.... They are all with us, except Bread, who is rather doubtful.... Light alone is on Man's side; but she won't come.... I made the children believe that they ought to steal away while she was asleep.... There never was such an opportunity.... (A murmuring in the leaves.) Ah, that's the Beech's voice!... Yes, you are right; we must inform the animals.... Has the Rabbit got his drum?... Is he with you?... Good, let him beat the troop at once.... Here they are!...

(The roll of the RABBIT'S *drum is heard, diminishing in the distance. Enter* TYLTYL, MYTYL *and the* DOG.)

TYLTYL
Is this the place?...

THE CAT (obsequiously, eagerly, mealy-mouthed, rushing to meet the CHILDREN)
Ah, there you are, my little master!... How well you look and how pretty, this evening!.... I went before you to announce your arrival.... All Is going well. We shall have the Blue Bird to-night, I am sure.... I have just sent the Rabbit to beat the troop in order to convoke the principal animals of the country.... You can hear them already among the foliage.... Listen!... They are a little shy and dare not come near.... (The sounds are heard of different animals, such as cows, pigs, horses, donkeys, etc. The CAT, *aside, to* TYLTYL, *taking him apart*) But why have you brought the Dog?... I have told you he is on the worst terms with everybody, even the trees.... I fear that his odious presence will spoil

everything....

TYLTYL
I could not get rid of him.... (To the DOG, **threatening him**)
Go away, you ugly thing!...

THE DOG
Who?... I?... Why?... What have I done?...

TYLTYL
I tell you, go away!... We don't want you here and there's an end of it....
You're a nuisance, there!...

THE DOG
I sha'n't say a word.... I shall follow you at a distance.... They sha'n't see me.... Shall I beg?...

THE CAT (aside, to TYLTYL)
Do you allow this disobedience?... Hit him on the nose with your stick; he is really unbearable!...

TYLTYL (beating the DOG)
There, that will teach you to be more obedient!...

THE DOG (yelling)
Ow! Ow! Ow!...

TYLTYL
What do you say?...

THE DOG
I must kiss you now you've beaten me!... (He covers TYLTYL **with violent kisses and embraces**.)

TYLTYL

Come.... That will do.... That's enough.... Go away!...

MYTYL

No, no; I want him to stay.... I am afraid of everything when he is not there....

THE DOG (leaping up and almost upsetting MYTYL, *whom he overwhelms with*

hurried and enthusiastic kisses)

Oh, the dear little girl!... How beautiful she is!... How good she is!... How beautiful she is, how sweet she is!...I must kiss her!... Once more, once more, once more!...

THE CAT

What an idiot!... Well, we shall see!... Let us lose no time.... Turn the diamond....

TYLTYL

Where shall I stand?...

THE CAT

In this moonbeam; you will see better.... There, turn it gently!...

(TYLTYL *turns the Diamond. A long-drawn-out rustling shakes the leaves and branches. The oldest and most stately trunks open to make way for the soul which each of them contains. The appearance of these souls differs according to the appearance and the character of the trees which they represent. The soul of the* ELM, *for instance, is a sort of pursy, pot-bellied, crabbed gnome; the* LIME-TREE *is placid, familiar and jovial; the* BEECH, *elegant and agile; the* BIRCH, *white, reserved and restless; the* WILLOW, *stunted, dishevelled and plaintive; the* FIR-TREE, *tall, lean and taciturn; the* CYPRESS, tragic; the CHESTNUT-TREE, *pretentious and rather dandified; the* POPLAR, *sprightly, cumbersome, talkative. Some emerge slowly from their trunks, torpidly stretching themselves, as though they had been imprisoned or asleep for ages; others leap out actively, eagerly; and all come and stand in a circle round the two* CHILDREN, *while keeping as near as they can to the tree in which they were born*.)

THE POPLAR (running up first and screaming at the top of his voice)
Men?... Little men!... We shall be able to talk to them!... We've done with silence!... Done with it!... Where do they come from?... Who are they?... What are they?... (To the LIME-TREE, *who comes forward quietly smoking his pipe*) Do you know them, Daddy Lime-Tree?...

THE LIME-TREE
I do not remember ever having seen them....

THE POPLAR
Oh, yes, you must have!... You know all the men; you're always hanging about their houses....

THE LIME-TREE (examining the CHILDREN)
No, I assure you.... I don't know them.... They are too young still.... I only know the lovers who come to see me by moonlight and the topers who drink their beer under my branches....

THE CHESTNUT-TREE (affectedly adjusting his eyeglass)
Who are these?... Are they poor people from the country?...

THE POPLAR
Oh, as for you, Mr. Chestnut-Tree, ever since you have refused to show yourself except in the streets of the big towns...

THE WILLOW (hobbling along in a pair of wooden shoes)
Oh dear, oh dear!... They have come to cut off my head and arms again for fagots!...

THE POPLAR
Silence!... Here is the Oak leaving his palace!... He looks far from well this evening.... Don't you think he is growing very old?... What can his age be?... The Fir-tree says he is four thousand; but I am sure that he exaggerates.... Listen; he will tell us all about it....

(The OAK *comes slowly forward. He is fabulously old, crowned with mistletoe and clad in a long green gown edged with moss and lichen. He is blind; his white beard streams in the wind. He leans with one hand on a knotty stick and with the other on a young* OAKLING, *who serves as his guide. The Blue Bird is perched on his shoulder. At his approach, the other trees draw themselves up in a row and bow respectfully*.)

TYLTYL
He has the Blue Bird!... Quick! Quick!... Here!... Give it to me!...

THE TREES
Silence!...

THE CAT (to TYLTYL)
Take of your hat. It's the Oak!...

THE OAK (to TYLTYL)
Who are you?....

TYLTYL
I am Tyltyl, sir.... When can I have the Blue Bird?...

THE OAK
Tyltyl, the wood-cutter's son?...

TYLTYL
Yes, sir....

THE OAK
Your father has done us much harm.... In my family alone, he has put to death six hundred of my sons, four hundred and seventy-five uncles and aunts, twelve hundred cousins of both sexes, three hundred and eighty daughters-in-law, and twelve thousand great-grandsons!...

TYLTYL
I know nothing about it, sir.... He did not do it on purpose....

THE OAK
What have you come here for; and why have you made our souls leave their abodes?...

TYLTYL
I beg your pardon, sir, for disturbing you.... The Cat said that you would tell us where the Blue Bird was....

THE OAK
Yes, I know that you are looking for the Blue Bird, that is to say, the great secret of things and of happiness, so that Man may make our servitude still harder....

TYLTYL
Oh, no, sir; it is for the Fairy Berylune's little girl, who is very ill....

THE OAK (laying silence upon him with a gesture)
Enough!... I do not hear the Animals.... Where are they?... All this concerns them as much as us.... We, the Trees, must not assume the responsibility alone for the grave measures that have become necessary.... On the day when MAN hears that we have done what we are about to do, there
will be terrible reprisals..... It is right, therefore, that our agreement should be unanimous, so that our silence may be the same....

THE FIR-TREE (looking over the top of the other trees)
The Animals are coming.... They are following the Rabbit.... Here are the souls of the Horse, the Bull, the Ox, the Cow, the Wolf, the Sheep, the Pig, the Cock, the Goat, the Ass, and the Bear....

(Enter the souls of the ANIMALS, *who, as the* FIR-TREE
utters their names, come forward and sit down among the trees, with the exception of the soul of the GOAT, *who roams to and fro, and of the* PIG, *who snuffles among the roots*.)

THE OAK
Are all here present?...

THE RABBIT
The Hen could not leave her eggs, the Hare is out on a run, the Stag has a pain in his horns, the Fox is ill--here is the doctor's certificate--the Goose did not understand and the Turkey flew into a passion....

THE OAK
These abstentions are most regrettable.... However, we have a quorum.... You know, my brothers, the nature of our business. The child you see before you, thanks to a talisman stolen from the powers of Earth, is able to take possession of the Blue Bird and thus to snatch from us the secret which we have kept since the origin of life.... Now we know enough of Man to

entertain no doubt as to the fate which he reserves for us once he is in possession of this secret. That is why it seems to me that any hesitation would be both foolish and criminal.... It is a serious moment; the child must be done away with before it is too late....

TYLTYL
What is he saying?...

THE DOG (prowling round the OAK *and showing his fangs*)
Do you see my teeth, you old cripple?...

THE BEECH (indignantly)
He is insulting the Oak!...

THE OAK
Is that the Dog?... Drive him out! We must suffer no traitors among us!...

THE CAT (aside, to TYLTYL)
Send the Dog away.... It's a misunderstanding.... Leave it to me; I will arrange things.... But send him away as quick as you can....

TYLTYL (to the DOG)
Will you be off!...

THE DOG
Do let me worry the gouty old beggar's moss slippers!.... It will be such a joke!...

TYLTYL
Hold your tongue!... And be off with you!... Be off, you ugly brute!...

THE DOG
All right, all right, I'm going.... I'll come back when you want me....

THE CAT (aside, to TYLTYL)
It would be a good thing to chain him up, or he will commit some folly; the Trees will be angry and all will end badly....

TYLTYL
What can I do?... I have lost his leash....

THE CAT
Here's the Ivy just coming along with strong bonds....

THE DOG (growling)
I'll come back, I'll come back!... Ugh! Goutytoes! Timbertoes!... Pack of old stunted growths, pack of old roots!... It's the Cat who's at the bottom of all this!... I'll be even with him!... What have you been whispering about, you sneak, you tiger, you Judas!... Wow, wow, wow!....

THE CAT
You see, he insults everybody....

TYLTYL
Yes, he is unbearable and one can't hear one's self speak.... Mr. Ivy, will you chain him up, please?...

THE IVY (timorously going up to the DOG)
Won't he bite?...

THE DOG (growling)
On the contrary, on the contrary!... He's going to kiss you!... Just wait and see!... Come along, come along, you old ball of twine, you!...

TYLTYL (threatening him with his stick)
Tylo!...

THE DOG (cringing at TYLTYL'S *feet and wagging his tail*)
What am I to do, my little god?

TYLTYL
Lie down flat!... Obey the Ivy.... Let him bind you, or....

THE DOG (growling between his teeth, while the IVY *binds him*)
Ball of twine I... Hunk of yarn!... Hangman's rope I... Calves' leash!... Look, my little god I ... He's cutting my paws!... He's choking me!...

TYLTYL
I don't care!... It's your own fault.... Hold your tongue; be quiet; you're unbearable!...

THE DOG
You're wrong, for all that.... They mean mischief.... Take care, my little god!... He's closing my mouth!... I can't speak!...

THE IVY (who has tied up the DOG *like a parcel*)
Where shall we put him?... I've muzzled him finely.... He can't utter a word....

THE OAK
Fasten him tight down there behind my trunk; to my big root.... We will decide later what had best be done with him....

(The IVY *and the* POPLAR *carry the* DOG *behind the* OAK'S *trunk*.)

THE OAK
Is that done?... Well, now that we are rid of this inconvenient witness, of this renegade, let us deliberate in accordance with justice and truth.... I will not conceal from you the deep and painful nature of my emotion....

This is the first time that it is given to us to judge Man and make him feel our power.... I do not think that, after the harm which he has done us, after the monstrous injustice which we have suffered, there can remain the least doubt as to the sentence that awaits him....

ALL THE TREES and ALL THE ANIMALS
No! No! No!... No doubt at all!... Hanging!... Death!... The injustice has been too great!... The abuse too wicked!... It has lasted too long!... Crush him!... Eat him!... At once!... Here and now!...

TYLTYL (to the CAT)
What is the matter with them?... Are they displeased?...

THE CAT
Don't be alarmed.... They are a little annoyed because Spring is late.... Leave it to me; I will settle it all....

THE OAK
This unanimity was inevitable.... We must now decide, in order to avoid reprisals, which form of execution will be the most practical, the easiest, the quickest and the safest, which will leave the fewest accusing traces when Man finds the little bodies in the forest....

TYLTYL
What is all this about?... What is he driving at?... I am getting tired of this.... He has got the Blue Bird; let him hand it over....

THE BULL (coming forward)
The most practical and the surest way is a good butt with the horns in the pit of the stomach.... Shall I go at him?...

THE OAK
Who speaks?...

THE CAT
It's the Bull.

THE COW
It would be better to keep quiet.... I won't meddle with it.... I have all the grass to browse in the field which you can see down there in the blue light of the moon.... I have quite enough to do....

THE OX
I also.... However, I agree to everything beforehand....

THE BEECH
I can offer my highest branch to hang them on....

THE IVY
And I the slip-knot....

THE FIR-TREE
And I the four planks for their little coffin....

THE CYPRESS
And I a perpetual grant of a tomb....

THE WILLOW
The simplest way would be to drown them in one of my rivers.... I will take charge of that....

THE LIME-TREE (in a conciliatory tone)
Come, come.... Is it really necessary to go to such extremities?... They are very young.... We could quite simply prevent them from doing any harm by keeping them prisoners in an enclosure which I will undertake to form by planting myself all around....

THE OAK
Who speaks?... I seem to recognise the honeyed accents of the Lime-tree....

THE FIR-TREE
Yes, it's he....

THE OAK
So there is a renegade among us, as among the Animals?... Hitherto we have only had to deplore the disloyalty of the Fruit-trees; but they are not real trees....

THE PIG (rolling his small eyes gluttonously)
I think we should first eat the little girl.... She ought to be very tender....

TYLTYL
What's he saying?... Just wait a bit, you...

THE CAT
I don't know what is the matter with them; but things are beginning to look badly....

THE OAK
Silence!... What we have to decide is which of us shall have the honour of striking the first blow, who shall ward off from, our tops the greatest danger that has threatened us since the birth of Man....

THE FIR-TREE
That honour falls to you, our king and our patriarch....

THE OAK
Is that the Fir-tree speaking?... Alas, I am too old!... I am blind and infirm and my numbed arms no longer obey me.... No, to you, brother, ever

green, ever upright, to you, who have witnessed the birth of most of these trees, to you be the glory, in default of myself, of the noble act of our deliverance....

THE FIR-TREE
I thank you, venerable father.... But as I shall, in any case, have the honour of burying the two victims, I should be afraid of arousing the just jealousy of my colleagues; and I think that, next to ourselves, the oldest and the worthiest and the one that owns the best club is the Beech....

THE BEECH
You know I am worm-eaten and my club is no longer to be relied upon.... But the Elm and the Cypress have powerful weapons....

THE ELM
I should be only too pleased; but I can hardly stand upright.... A mole twisted my great toe last night....

THE CYPRESS
As for me, I am ready.... But, like my brother, the Fir-tree, I shall have, if not the privilege of burying them, at least the advantage of weeping over their tomb.... It would be an unlawful plurality of offices.... Ask the Poplar....

THE POPLAR
Me?... Are you serious?... Why, my wood is more tender than the flesh of a child!... And, besides, I don't know what's the matter with me.... I am shivering with fever.... Just look at my leaves.... I must have caught cold at sunrise this morning....

THE OAK (bursting out with indignation)
You are afraid of Man!... Even those unprotected and unarmed little children inspire you with the mysterious terror which has always made us

the slaves that we are!... Enough of this! Things being as they are and the opportunity unequalled, I shall go forth alone, old, crippled, trembling, blind as I am, against the hereditary enemy!... Where is he?...

(Groping with his stick, he moves towards TYLTYL.)

TYLTYL (taking his knife from his pocket)
Is it me he's after, that old one, with his big stick?...

ALL THE TREES (uttering a cry of alarm at the sight of the knife, they step in between and hold back the OAK)
The knife!... Take care!... The knife!...

THE OAK (struggling)
Let me be!... What does it matter?... The knife or the axe!... Who's holding me back?... What! Are you all here?... What! You all want to.... (Flinging down his *stick*) Well, so be it!... Shame upon us!... Let the Animals deliver us!...

THE BULL
That's right!... I'll see to It!... And with one blow of the horns!...

THE OX *and* THE COW (holding him back by the tail)
What are you doing?... Don't be a fool!... It's a bad business!... It will end badly.... It is we who will pay for it.... Do let be.... It's the wild animals' business....

THE BULL
No, no!... It's my business!... Wait and see!... Look here, hold me back or there will be an accident!...

TYLTYL (to MYTYL, **who is uttering piercing screams**)
Don't be afraid!... Stand behind me.... I have my knife....

THE COCK
He has plenty of pluck, the little chap!...

TYLTYL
So you've made up your minds, it's me you're going for?...

THE ASS
Why, of course, my little man; you've taken long enough to see it!...

THE PIG
You can say your prayers; your last hour has come.... But don't hide the little girl.... I want to feast my eyes on her.... I'm going to eat her first....

TYLTYL
What have I done to you?...

THE SHEEP
Nothing at all, my little man.... Eaten my little brother, my two sisters, my three uncles, my aunt, my grandpapa and my grandmamma.... Wait, wait, when you're down, you shall see that I have teeth also....

THE ASS
And I hoofs!...

THE HORSE (haughtily pawing the ground)
You shall see what you shall see!... Would you rather that I tore you with my teeth or knocked you down with a kick?... (He moves ostentatiously towards TYLTYL, *who faces him and raises his knife. Suddenly the* HORSE, *seized with panic, turns and rushes away*.) Ah, no!... That's not fair!... That's against the rules!.... He's defending himself!...

THE COCK (unable to hide his admiration)
I don't care, the little chap's full of grit!...

THE PIG (to the BEAR *and the* WOLF)
Let us all rush on them together.... I will support you from the rear.... We will throw them down and share the little girl when she is on the ground....

THE WOLF
Divert their attention in front.... I am going to make a turning movement....

(He goes round TYLTYL, *whom he attacks from behind and half overthrows*.)

TYLTYL
You brute!... (He raises himself on one knee brandishing his knife and doing his best to cover his little sister, who utters yells of distress. Seeing him half overturned, all the ANIMALS *and* TREES *come up and try to hit him*. TYLTYL *calls distractedly for assistance*.)
Help! Help!... Tylo! Tylo!... Where is the Cat?... Tylo!... Tylette! Tylette!... Come! Come!...

THE CAT (hypocritically, holding aloof)
I can't come.... I have sprained my paw....

TYLTYL (warding of the blows and defending himself as best he can)
Help!... Tylo! Tylo!... I can't hold out!... There are too many of them!... The Bear! The Pig! The Donkey! The Ass! The Fir-tree! The Beech!... Tylo! Tylo! Tylo!...

(*Dragging his broken bonds after him, the* DOG *leaps from behind the trunk of the* OAK *and, elbowing his way through* TREES *and* ANIMALS, *flings himself before* TYLTYL, *whom he defends furiously*.)

THE DOG (distributing great bites)
Here! Here, my little god!... Don't be afraid! Have at them!... I know how to use my teeth!... Here, there's one for you, Bear, in your fat hams!... Now then, who wants some more?... Here, that's for the Pig and that's for the Horse and that's for the Bull's tail!... There, I've torn the Beech's trousers and the Oak's petticoat!... The Fir-tree's making tracks!... Whew, it's warm work!...

TYLTYL (overcome)
I'm done for!... The Cypress has caught me a great blow on the head....

THE DOG
Ow!... That's the Willow!... He's broken my paw!...

TYLTYL
They're coming back, they're charging down upon us, all together!... This time, it's the Wolf!...

THE DOG
Wait till I give him one for himself!...

THE WOLF
Fool!... Our brother!... His father drowned your seven puppies!...

THE DOG
Quite right!... And a good thing too!... It was because they looked like you!...

ALL THE TREES AND ANIMALS
Renegade!... Idiot!... Traitor!... Felon!... Simpleton!... Judas!... Leave him!... He's a dead man!... Come over to us!...

THE DOG (drunk with ardour and devotion)
Never! Never!... I alone against all of you!... Never! Never!... True to the gods, to the best, to the greatest!... (To TYLTYL) Take care, here's the Bear!... Beware of the Bull!... I'll jump at his throat.... Ow!... That's a kick.... The Ass has broken two of my teeth....

TYLTYL
I'm done for, Tylo!... Ah!... That was a blow from the Elm.... Look, my hand's bleeding.... That's the Wolf or the Pig....

THE DOG
Wait, my little god.... Let me kiss you.... There, a good lick.... That will do you good.... Keep behind me.... They dare not come again.... Yes, though.... Here they are coming back!... This time, it's serious!.... We must stand firm!...

TYLTYL (dropping to the ground)
No, I can hold out no longer!...

THE DOG (listening)
They are coming!... I hear them, I scent them!...

TYLTYL
Where?... Who?...

THE DOG
There! There!... It's Light!... She has found us!... Saved, my little king!... Kiss me!... We are saved!... Look!... They're alarmed!... They're retreating!... They're afraid!...

TYLTYL
Light!... Light!... Come quick!... Hurry!... They have rebelled!... They are all against us!...

Enter LIGHT. *As she comes forward, the dawn rises over the forest, which becomes light*.

LIGHT
What is it?... What has happened?... But, my poor boy, didn't you know?... Turn the diamond!... They will return into silence and obscurity; and you will no longer perceive their hidden feelings....

(TYLTYL *turns the diamond. Immediately, the souls of all the* TREES rush back into the trunks, which close again. The souls of the ANIMALS *also disappear; and a peaceful* COW *and* SHEEP, etc., are seen browsing in the distance. The Forest becomes harmless once more, TYLTYL *looks around him in amazement*.)

TYLTYL
Where are they?... What was the matter with them?... Were they mad?...

LIGHT
No, they are always like that; but we do not know it because we do not see it.... I told you so before; it is dangerous to wake them when I am not there....

TYLTYL (wiping his knife)
Well, but for the Dog and if I had not had my knife!... I would never have believed that they were so wicked!...

LIGHT
You see that Man is all alone against all in this world....

THE DOG
Are you very badly hurt, my little god?....

TYLTYL
Nothing serious.... As for Mytyl, they have not touched her.... But you, my dear Tylo?... Your mouth is all over blood and your paw is broken!...

THE DOG
It is not worth speaking of.... It won't show to-morrow.... But it was a tough fight!...

THE CAT (appearing from behind a thicket, limping)
I should think so!... The Ox caught me a blow with his horns in the stomach.... You can't see the marks, but it's very painful.... And the Oak broke my paw....

THE DOG
I should like to know which one....

MYTYL (stroking the CAT)
My poor Tylette, did he really?.... Where were you?... I did not see you....

THE CAT (hypocritically)
Mummy dear, I was wounded at the first, while attacking that horrid Pig, who wanted to eat you.... And then the Oak gave me a great blow which struck me senseless....

THE DOG (to the CAT, **between his teeth**)
As for you, I want a word with you presently.... It will keep!...

THE CAT (plaintively, to MYTYL)
Mummy dear, he's insulting me.... He wants to hurt me....

MYTYL (to the DOG)
Leave him alone, will you, you ugly beast?...

(They all go out.)

CURTAIN

ACT IV

SCENE 1.--Before the Curtain.

The curtain represents beautiful clouds

(Enter TYLTYL, MYTYL, LIGHT, *the* DOG, *the* CAT, BREAD, FIRE, SUGAR, WATER *and* MILK.)

LIGHT
I believe we have the Blue Bird this time. I ought to have thought of it before. But the idea came to me, like a ray from the sky, this morning only, when I recovered my strengthen the dawn.... We are at the entrance to the enchanted palaces where all men's Joys, all men's Happinesses are gathered together in the charge of Fate.

TYLTYL
Are there many of them? Shall we have any? Are they little?

LIGHT
Some are little and some are great; some are coarse and some are delicate; some are very beautiful and others not so pleasant to look upon.... But the ugliest were expelled from the garden some time ago and took refuge with the Miseries. For we must not forget that the Miseries inhabit an adjoining

cave, which communicates with the Garden of Happiness and is separated from it only by a sort of vapour or fine veil, lifted at every moment by the winds that blow from the heights of Justice or from the depths of Eternity.... What we have now to do is to organise ourselves and take certain precautions. Generally, the Joys are very good; but, still, there are some of them that are more dangerous and treacherous than the greatest Miseries.

BREAD
I have an idea! If they are dangerous and treacherous, would it not be better for us all to wait at the door, so that we may lend a hand to the children should they be obliged to fly?....

THE DOG
Not at all! Not at all! I mean to go everywhere with my little gods! Let those who are afraid remain at the door! We have no need (looking at BREAD) of cowards (looking at the CAT) or traitors!...

FIRE
I'm going!... I hear it's great fun!... They dance all the time....

BREAD
Do they have any eating as well?

WATER (moaning)
I have never known the smallest Happiness!... I should like to see some at last!....

LIGHT
Hold your tongues! Who asked your opinions?... This is what I have decided: the Dog, Bread and Sugar shall go with the children. Water shall stay outside, because she is too cold, and Fire, because he is too turbulent. I strongly urge Milk to remain at the door, because he is so impressionable.

As for the Cat, he can do as he likes.....

THE CAT
I shall take the opportunity of calling on the chief Miseries of my acquaintance, who live next door to the Joys....

TYLTYL
And you, Light? Aren't you coming?

LIGHT
I cannot go into the Joys like this: most of them cannot endure me. But I have here the thick veil with which I cover myself when I visit happy people.... (She unfolds a long veil and wraps herself in it carefully.) Not a ray of my you! must startle them, for there are many Happinesses that are afraid and are not happy.... There... like this, even the ugliest and coarsest of them will have nothing to fear....

(The curtain opens and discloses the next Scene)

SCENE 2.--The Palace of Happiness.

When the curtain of clouds opens, the stage represents, in the forefront of the palace, a sort of hall formed of tall marble columns, between which hang heavy purple draperies, supported by golden ropes and concealing all the background. The architecture suggests the most sensual and sumptuous moments of the Venetian or Flemish Renascence, as seen in the pictures of Veronese or Rubens, with garlands, horns of plenty, fringes, vases, statues, gildings, lavishly distributed on every side. In the middle stands a massive and marvellous table of jasper and silver-gilt, laden with candlesticks, glass, gold and silver plate and fabulous viands. Around the table, the biggest luxuries of the Earth sit eating, drinking, shouting, singing, tossing and lolling about or sleeping among the haunches of venison, the miraculous fruits, the overturned jars and ewers. They are enormously, incredibly fat and red in the face, covered with velvet and brocade, crowned with gold and pearls and precious stones. Beautiful female slaves incessantly bring decorated dishes and foaming beverages. Vulgar, blatantly hilarious music, in which the brasses predominate. The stage is bathed in a red and heavy light.

(TYLTYL, MYTYL, *the* DOG, BREAD *and* SUGAR *are a little awestruck at first end crowd round* LIGHT *in the foreground, to the right. The* CAT, *without a word, walks to the background, also to the right, lifts a dark curtain and disappears*.)

TYLTYL
Who are those fat gentlemen enjoying themselves and eating such a lot of good things?

LIGHT
They are the biggest Luxuries of the Earth, the ones that can be seen with

the naked eye. It is possible, though not very likely, that the Blue Bird may have strayed among them for a moment. That is why you must not turn the diamond yet. For form's sake, we will begin by searching this part of the hall.

TYLTYL
Can we go up to them?

LIGHT
Certainly. They are not ill-natured, although they are vulgar and usually rather ill-bred.

MYTYL
What beautiful cakes they have!....

THE DOG
And such game! And sausages! And legs of lamb and calves' liver!... There is nothing nicer or lovelier in the world than liver!...

BREAD
Except quartern-loaves made of fine white flour! They have splendid ones!... How lovely they are! How lovely they are!...

SUGAR
I beg your pardon, I beg your pardon, I beg a thousand pardons.... Allow me, allow me.... I would not like to hurt anybody's feelings; but are you not forgetting the sweetmeats, which form the glory of that table and which, if I may say so, surpass in grandeur and magnificence all that exists in this hall, or perhaps anywhere else?...

TYLTYL
How pleased and happy they look!... And they are shouting! And laughing! And singing!... I believe they have seen us....

*(A dozen of the biggest LUXURIES **have risen from table and now, holding their stomachs in their hands, advance laboriously towards the** CHILDREN.)*

LIGHT
Have no fear, they are very affable.... They will probably invite you to dinner.... Do not accept, do not accept anything, lest you should forget your mission....

TYLTYL
What? Not even a tiny cake? They look so good, so fresh, so well iced with sugar, covered with candied fruits and brimming over with cream!...

LIGHT
They are dangerous and would break your will. A man should know how to sacrifice something to the duty he is performing. Refuse politely, but firmly.

THE BIGGEST OF THE LUXURIES (holding out his hand to TYLTYL)
How do you do, Tyltyl?...

TYLTYL (surprised)
Why, do you know me?... Who are you?...

THE LUXURY
I am the biggest of the Luxuries, the Luxury of Being Rich; and I come, in the name of my brothers, to beg you and your family to honour our endless repast with your presence. You will find yourself surrounded by all that is best among the real, big Luxuries of this Earth. Allow me to introduce to you the chief of them. Here is my son-in-law, the Luxury of Being a Landowner, who has a stomach shaped like a pear. This is the Luxury of Satisfied Vanity, who has such a nice, puffy face, (The LUXURY OF SATISFIED VANITY *gives a patronising nod*.) These are the Luxury of

Drinking when you are not Thirsty and the Luxury of Eating when you are not Hungry: they are twins and their legs are made of macaroni. (They bow, staggering.) Here are the Luxury of Knowing Nothing, who is as deaf as a post, and the Luxury of Understanding Nothing, who is as blind as a bat. Here are the Luxury of Doing Nothing and the Luxury of Sleeping more than Necessary: their hands are made of bread-crumb and their eyes of peach-jelly. Lastly, here is Fat Laughter: his mouth is split from ear to ear and he is irresistible....

(FAT LAUGHTER *bows, writhing and holding his sides*.)

TYLTYL (pointing to a LUXURY *who is standing a little on one side*)
And who is that one, who dares not come up to us and who is turning his back?...

THE LUXURY OF BEING RICH
Do not ask about him: he is a little awkward and is not fit to be introduced to children.... (Seizing TYLTYL'S *hands*) But come along! They are beginning the banquet all over again.... It is the twelfth time since this morning. We are only waiting for you.... Do you hear all the revellers calling and shouting for you?... I cannot introduce you to all of them, there are so many of them.... (Offering his arm to the two children) Allow me to lead you to the two seats of honour....

TYLTYL
No, thank you very much, Mr. Luxury.... I am so sorry.... I can't come for the moment.... We are in a great hurry, we are looking for the Blue Bird. You don't happen to know, I suppose, where he is hiding?

THE LUXURY
The Blue Bird?... Wait a bit.... Yes, I remember.... Some one was telling me about him the other day.... He is a bird, that is not good to eat, I believe.... At any rate, he has never figured on our table.... That means

that we have a poor opinion of him. But don't trouble; we have much better things…. You shall share our life, you shall see all that we do….

TYLTYL
What do you do?

THE LUXURY
Why, we occupy ourselves incessantly in doing nothing…. We never have a moment's rest…. We have to drink, we have to eat, we have to sleep. It's most engrossing….

TYLTYL
Is it amusing?

THE LUXURY
Why, yes…. It needs must be; it's all there is on this Earth….

LIGHT
Do you think so?...

THE LUXURY (pointing to LIGHT, *aside, to* TYLTYL)
Who is that ill-bred young person?...

(During the whole of the preceding conversation a crowd of LUXURIES of the second order have been busying themselves with the DOG, SUGAR **and** BREAD **and have dragged them to the orgie**. TYLTYL suddenly sees them seated fraternally at the table with their hosts, eating, drinking and flinging themselves about wildly.)

TYLTYL
Why, look, Light!... They are sitting at the table!...

LIGHT
Call them back, or this will have a bad end!...

TYLTYL
Tylo!... Here, Tylo!... Come here at once, will you? Do you hear?... And you too, Sugar and Bread, who told you to leave me?... What are you doing there, without permission?

BREAD (speaking with his mouth full)
Can't you keep a civil tongue in your mouth?...

TYLTYL
What? Is Bread daring to be impertinent?... Why, what's come over you?... And you, Tylo?... Is that the way you obey? Now then, come here, on your knees, on your knees!... And look sharp!...

THE DOG (muttering, from the end of the table)
When I'm eating, I'm at home to nobody and I hear nothing....

SUGAR (honey-mouthed)
Pardon us, we could not possibly leave such charming hosts so abruptly: they would be offended....

THE LUXURY
You see!... They are setting you an example.... Come, we are waiting for you.... We won't hear of a refusal.... We shall have to resort to a gentle violence.... Come, you Luxuries, help me!... Let us push them to the table by force, so that they may be happy in spite of themselves!... (All the LUXURIES, *uttering cries of joy and skipping about as nimbly as they are able, drag the* CHILDREN, *who struggle, while* FAT LAUGHTER *seizes* LIGHT *vigorously round the waist*.)

LIGHT

Turn the diamond, it is time!...

(TYTLYL *obeys* LIGHT'S *order. Forthwith, the stage is lit up with an ineffably pure, divinely roseate, harmonious and ethereal brightness. The heavy ornaments in the foreground, the thick red hangings become unfastened and disappear, revealing an immense and magnificent hall, a sort of cathedral of gladness and serenity, tall, innocent and almost transparent, whose endless fabric rests upon innumerous long and slender, limpid and blissful columns, suggesting the architecture of the Palladian churches or certain drawings by Carpaccio, notably the "Presentation of the Virgin" in the Uffizi Gallery. The table of the orgie melts away without leaving a trace; the velvets, the brocades, the garlands of the* LUXURIES *rise before the luminous gust that invades the temple tear asunder and fall, together with the grinning masks, at the feet of the astounded revellers. These become visibly deflated, like burst bladders, exchange glances, blink their eyes in the unknown rays that hurt them; and, seeing themselves at last as they really are, that is to say, naked, hideous, flabby and lamentable, they begin to utter yells of shame and dismay, amid which those of* FAT LAUGHTER *are clearly distinguishable above all the rest. The* LUXURY OF UNDERSTANDING NOTHING *alone remains perfectly calm, while his friends rush about madly, trying to flee, to hide themselves in corners which they hope to find dark. But there is not a shadow left in the dazzling room. And so the majority, in their despair, decide to pass through the threatening curtain which, in an angle on the right, closes the vault of the Cave of Miseries. Each time that one of them, in his panic, raises a skirt of the curtain, a storm of oaths, imprecations and maledictions is heard to issue from the hollow depths of the cave. As for the* DOG, BREAD *and* SUGAR, *they hang their heads, join the group of the* CHILDREN *and hide behind them very sheepishly*.)

TYLTYL (watching the LUXURIES *flying*)
Goodness, how ugly they are!... Where are they going?...

LIGHT
I really believe that they have lost their heads.... They are going to take refuge with the Miseries, where I very much fear that they will be kept for good....

TYLTYL (looking around him, wonder-struck)
Oh, what a beautiful hall, what a beautiful hall!... Where are we?...

LIGHT
We have not moved: it is your eyes that see differently.... We now behold the truth of things; and we shall perceive the soul of the Joys that endure the brightness of the diamond.

TYLTYL
How beautiful it is!... And what lovely weather!... It is just like midsummer.... Hullo! It looks as though people were coming to talk to us....

(The halls begin to fill with angel forms that seem to be emerging from a long slumber and glide harmoniously between the columns. They are clad in shimmering dresses, of soft and subtle shades; rose-awakening, water's-smile, amber-dew, blue-of-dawn, etc.)

LIGHT
Here come some amiable and curious Joys who will direct us....

TYLTYL
Do you know them?...

LIGHT

Yes, I know them all; I often come to them, without their knowing who I am....

TYLTYL

Oh, what a lot of them there are!... They are crowding from every side!

LIGHT

There were many more of them once. The Luxuries have done them great harm.

TYLTYL

No matter, there are a good few of them left....

LIGHT

You will see plenty of others, as the influence of the diamond spreads through the halls.... There are many more Happinesses on Earth than people think; but the generality of men do not discover them....

TYLTYL

Here are some little ones: let us run and meet them....

LIGHT

It is unnecessary: those which interest us will pass this way. We have no time to make the acquaintance of all the rest....

(A troop of little HAPPINESSES, *frisking and bursting with laughter, run up from the back of the halls and dance round the* CHILDREN *in a ring*.)

TYLTYL

How pretty, how very pretty they are!... Where do they come from, who are they?...

LIGHT
They are the Children's Happinesses....

TYLTYL
Can one speak to them?

LIGHT
It would be no use. They sing, they dance, they laugh, but they do not talk yet....

TYLTYL (skipping about)
How do you do? How do you do?... Oh, look at that fat one laughing!... What pretty cheeks they have, what pretty frocks they have!... Are they all rich here?...

LIGHT
Why, no, here, as everywhere, there are many more poor than rich....

TYLTYL
Where are the poor ones?...

LIGHT
You can't distinguish them.... A Child's Happiness is always arrayed in all that is most beautiful in Heaven and upon Earth.

TYLTYL (unable to restrain himself)
I should like to dance with them....

LIGHT
It is absolutely impossible, we have no time.... I see that they have not the Blue Bird.... Besides, they are in a hurry: you see, they have already passed.... They too have no time to waste, for childhood is very short....

(Another troop of HAPPINESSES, *a little taller than the last, rush into the hall, singing at the top of their voice, "There they are! There they are! They see us! They see us!" and, dance a merry fling around the* CHILDREN, *at the end of which the one who appears to be the chief of the little band goes up to* TYLTYL *with hand outstretched*.)

THE HAPPINESS
How do you do, Tyltyl?...

TYLTYL
Another one who knows me!... (To LIGHT) I am getting known wherever I go!... (To the HAPPINESS) Who are you?...

THE HAPPINESS
Don't you recognise me?... I'll wager that you don't recognise any one here!

TYLTYL (a little embarrassed)
Why, no.... I don't know.... I don't remember seeing any of you.

THE HAPPINESS
There, do you hear?... I was sure of it!... He has never seen us!...

(All the other HAPPINESSES *burst out laughing*) Why, my dear Tyltyl, we are the only things you do know!... We are always around you!... We eat, drink, wake up, breathe and live with you!...

TYLTYL
Oh, yes, just so, I know, I remember.... But I should like to know what your names are....

THE HAPPINESS
I can see that you know nothing.... I am the chief of the Happinesses of your home; and all these are the other Happinesses that live there....

TYLTYL
Then there are Happinesses in my home?

(All the HAPPINESSES *burst out laughing*.)

THE HAPPINESS
You heard him!... Are there Happinesses in his home!... Why, you little wretch, it is crammed with Happinesses in every nook and cranny!... We laugh, we sing, we create enough joy to knock down the walls and lift the roof; but, do what we may, you see nothing and you hear nothing.... I hope that, in future, you will be a little more sensible.... Meantime, you shall shake hands with the more noteworthy of us.... Then, when you reach home again, you will recognise them more easily and, at the end of a fine day, you will know how to encourage them with a smile, to thank them with a pleasant word, for they really do all they can to make your life easy and delightful.... Let me introduce myself first: the Happiness of Being Well, at your service.... I am not the prettiest, but I am the most important. Will you know me again?... This is the Happiness of Pure Air, who is almost transparent.... Here is the Happiness of Loving one's Parents, who is clad in grey and always a little sad, because no one ever looks at him.... Here are the Happiness of the Blue Sky. who, of course, is dressed in blue, and the Happiness of the Forest, who, also of course, is clad in green: you will see him every time you go to the window.... Here, again, is the good Happiness of Sunny Hours, who is diamond-coloured, and this is the Happiness of Spring, who is bright emerald....

TYLTYL
And are you as fine as that every day?

THE HAPPINESS OF BEING WELL
Why, yes, it is Sunday every day, in every house, when people open their eyes.... And then, when evening comes, here is the Happiness of the Sunsets, who is grander than all the kings in the world and who is followed by the Happiness of Seeing the Stars Rise, who is gilded like a god of old.... Then, when the weather breaks, here are the Happiness of the Rain, who is covered with pearls, and the Happiness of the Winter Fire, who opens his beautiful purple mantle to frozen hands.... And I have not mentioned the best among us, because he is nearly a brother of the great limpid Joys whom you will see presently: his name is the Happiness of Innocent Thoughts, and he is the brightest of as all.... And then here are.... But really there are too many of them!... We should never have done; and I must first send word to the Great Joys, who are right at the back, near the gates of Heaven, and who have not yet heard of your arrival.... I will send the Happiness of Running Barefoot in the Dew, who is the nimblest of us.... (To the HAPPINESS OF RUNNING BAREFOOT IN THE DEW, *who comes forward capering*) Off you go!...

LIGHT (to TYLTYL)
In the meantime, you might enquire about the Blue Bird. It is just possible that the chief Happiness of your home knows where he is....

TYLTYL
Where Is he?...

THE HAPPINESS
He doesn't know where the Blue Bird is!... (All the HAPPINESSES OF THE HOME *burst out laughing*.)

TYLTYL (vexed)
No, I do not know.... There's nothing to laugh at.... (Fresh bursts of laughter.)

THE HAPPINESS
Come, don't be angry... and let us be serious.... He doesn't know: well, what do you expect? He is no more absurd than the majority of men.... But little Happiness of Running Barefoot in the Dew has told the Great Joys and they are coming towards us....

(Tall and beautiful angelic figures, clad in shimmering dresses, come slowly forward.)

TYLTYL
How beautiful they are!... Why are they not laughing?... Are they not happy?...

LIGHT
It is not when one laughs that one is really happy....

TYLTYL
Who are they?...

THE HAPPINESS
They are the Great Joys....

TYLTYL
Do you know their names?...

THE HAPPINESS
Of course; we often play with them.... Here, first of all, before the others, is the Great Joy of Being Just, who smiles each time an injustice is repaired. I am too young: I have never seen her smile yet. Behind her is the Joy of Being Good, who is the happiest, but the saddest; and it is very difficult to keep her from going to the Miseries, whom she would like to console; for, if she left us, we should be almost as miserable as the Miseries themselves. On the right is the Joy of Fame, next to the Joy of

Thinking. After her comes the Joy of Understanding, who is always looking for her brother, the Luxury of Understanding Nothing....

TYLTYL
But I have seen her brother!... He went to the Miseries with the Big Luxuries....

THE HAPPINESS
I was certain of it.... He has turned out badly; keeping evil company has corrupted him entirely.... But do not speak of it to his sister. She would want to go and look for him and we should lose one of our most beautiful Joys.... Here, among the greatest Joys, is the Joy of Seeing what is Beautiful, who daily adds a few rays to the light that reigns amongst us....

TYLTYL
And there, far away, far away, in the golden clouds, the one whom I can hardly see when I stand as high as I can on tip-toe?...

THE HAPPINESS
That is the Great Joy of Loving.... But, do what you will, you are ever so much too small to see her altogether....

TYLTYL
And over there, right at the back, those who are veiled and who do not come near?...

THE HAPPINESS
Those are the Joys whom men do not yet know....

TYLTYL
What do the others want with us?... Why are they standing aside?...

THE HAPPINESS
It is before a new Joy who is arriving, perhaps the purest that we have here....

TYLTYL
Who is it?

THE HAPPINESS
Don't you recognise her yet?... But take a better look at her, open your two eyes down to the very heart of your soul!... She has seen you, she has seen you!... She runs up to you, holding out her arms!... It is your mother's Joy, it is the peerless Joy of Maternal Love!...

(The other JOYS, *who have run up from every side, acclaim the* JOY OF MATERNAL LOVE *with their cheers and then fall back before her in*
silence.)

THE JOY OF MATERNAL LOVE
Tyltyl! And Mytyl!... What, do I find you here?... I never expected it!... I was very lonely at home; and here are you two climbing to that Heaven where the souls of all mothers beam with joy!... But first kisses, heaps and heaps of kisses!... Into my arms, the two of you; there is nothing on earth that gives greater happiness!... Tyltyl, aren't you laughing?... Nor you either, Mytyl?... Don't you know your mother's love when you see it?... Why, look at me: are these not my eyes, my lips, my arms?...

TYLTYL
Yes, yes, I recognise them, but I did not know.... You are like Mummy, but you are much prettier....

MATERNAL LOVE
Why, of course, I have stopped growing old.... And every day brings me

fresh strength and youth and happiness.... Each of your smiles makes me younger by a year.... At home, that does not show; but here everything is seen and it is the truth....

TYLTYL (wonder-struck, gazing at her and kissing her by turns)
And that beautiful dress of yours: what is it made of?... Is it silk, silver or pearls?...

MATERNAL LOVE
No, it is made of kisses and caresses and loving looks.... Each kiss you give me adds a ray of moon-light or sunshine to it....

TYLTYL
How funny, I should never have thought that you were so rich!... Where used you to hide it?... Was it in the cupboard of which Daddy has the key?...

MATERNAL LOVE
No, no, I always wear it, but people do not see it, because people see nothing when their eyes are closed.... All mothers are rich when they love their children.... There are no poor mothers, no ugly ones, no old ones. Their love is always the most beautiful of the Joys.... And, when they seem most sad, it needs but a kiss which they receive or give to turn all their tears into stars in the depths of their eyes....

TYLTYL (looking at her with astonishment)
Why, yes, it's true, your eyes are filled with stars.... And they are really your eyes, only they are much more beautiful.... And this is your hand too, with the little ring on it.... It even has the burn which you gave it one evening when lighting the lamp.... But it is much whiter; and how delicate the skin is!... There seems to be light flowing through it.... Doesn't it do any work like the one at home?...

MATERNAL LOVE

Why yes, it is the very same: did you never see that it becomes quite white and fills with light the moment it fondles you?...

TYLTYL

It's wonderful, Mummy: you have the same voice also; but you speak much better than you do at home....

MATERNAL LOVE

At home, one has too much to do and there is no time.... But what one does not say one hears all the same.... Now that you have seen me, will you know me again, in my torn dress, when you go back to the cottage tomorrow?...

TYLTYL

I don't want to go back.... As you are here, I want to stay also, as long as you remain....

MATERNAL LOVE

But it's just the same thing: I am down below, we are all down below.... You have come up here only to realise and to learn, once and for all, how to see me when you see me down below.... Do you understand, Tyltyl dear?... You believe yourself in Heaven; but Heaven is wherever you and I kiss each other.... There are not two mothers; and you have no other.... Every child has only one; and it is always the same one and always the most beautiful; but you have to know her and to know how to look.... But how did you manage
to come up here and to find a road for which men have been seeking ever since they began to dwell upon the Earth?...

TYLTYL (pointing to LIGHT, **who, discreetly, has drawn a little to one side**)
She brought me....

MATERNAL LOVE
Who is she?...

TYLTYL
Light....

MATERNAL LOVE
I have never seen her.... I was told that she was very fond of you both and very kind.... But why does she hide herself?... Does she never show her face?...

TYLTYL
Oh, yes, but she is afraid that the Joys might be frightened if they saw too clearly....

MATERNAL LOVE
But doesn't she know that we are waiting only for her! (Calling the other GREAT JOYS) Come, come, sisters! Come quickly, all of you! Light has come to visit us at last!...

(A stir among the GREAT JOYS, *who draw nearer, with cries of "Light is here!... Light! Light!..."*)

THE JOY OF UNDERSTANDING (thrusting all the others aside, to come and embrace LIGHT)
You are Light and we did not know it!... And we have been waiting for you for years and years and years!... Do you recognise me?... I am the Joy of Understanding, who have been seeking you for so long!... We are very happy, but we cannot see beyond ourselves....

THE JOY OF BEING JUST (embracing LIGHT *in her turn*)
Do you recognise me?... I am the Joy of Being Just, who have besought you so long.... We are very happy, but we cannot see beyond our shadows.

THE JOY OF SEEING WHAT IS BEAUTIFUL (also embracing LIGHT)
Do you recognise me?... I am the Joy of Seeing what is Beautiful, who have loved you so dearly.... We are very happy, but we cannot see beyond our dreams....

THE JOY OF UNDERSTANDING
Come, sister, come, do not keep us waiting any longer.... We are strong enough, we are pure enough.... Put aside those veils which still conceal from us the last truths and the last happinesses.... See, all my sisters are kneeling at your feet.... You are our queen and our reward.

LIGHT (drawing her veils closer)
Sisters, my beautiful sisters, I am obeying my Master.... The hour is not yet come; it will strike, perhaps, and I shall return without fear and without shadow.... Farewell, rise and let us kiss once more, like sisters lost and found, while waiting for the day that will soon appear....

MATERNAL LOVE (embracing LIGHT)
You have been very good to my poor little ones....

LIGHT
I shall always be good to those who love one another....

THE JOY OF UNDERSTANDING (going up to LIGHT)
Let the last kiss be laid upon my forehead....

(They exchange a long kiss; and, when they separate and raise their heads, tears are seen to stand in their eyes.)

TYLTYL (surprised)
Why are you crying?... (Looking at the other JOYS) I say! You're crying too!... But why have all of you tears in your eyes?...

LIGHT
Hush, dear....

CURTAIN

ACT V

SCENE I.--Before the Curtain.

Enter TYLTYL, MYTYL, LIGHT, *the* DOG, *the* CAT, BREAD, FIRE, SUGAR, WATER *and* MILK.

LIGHT
I have received a note from the Fairy Berylune telling me that the Blue Bird is probably here.

TYLTYL
Where?...

LIGHT
Here, in the graveyard behind that wall.... It appears that one of the dead in the graveyard is hiding it in his tomb.... We must find out which one it is.... We shall have to pass them under review....

TYLTYL
Under review?... How is that done?...

LIGHT
It is very simple: at midnight, so as not to disturb them too greatly, you

will turn the diamond. We shall see them come out of the ground; or else we shall see those who do not come out lying in their tombs....

TYLTYL
Will they not be angry?...

LIGHT
Not at all; they will not even know.... They do not like being disturbed, but, as it is their custom, in any case, to come out at midnight, that will not inconvenience them....

TYLTYL
Why are Bread, Sugar and Milk so pale and why do they say nothing?...

MILK (staggering)
I feel I am going to turn....

LIGHT (aside to TYLTYL)
Do not mind them.... They are afraid of the dead....

FIRE (frisking about)
I'm not afraid of them!... I am used to burning them.... Time was when I burnt them all; that was much more amusing than nowadays ...

TYLTYL
And why Is Tylo trembling?... Is he afraid, too?...

THE DOG
I?... I'm not trembling!... I am never afraid; but if you went away, I should go too....

TYLTYL
And has the Cat nothing to say?...

THE CAT (mysteriously)
I know what's what....

TYLTYL (to LIGHT)
Are you coming with us?...

LIGHT
No; it is better that I should remain at the gate of the graveyard with the Things and the Animals.... Some of them would be too frightened and I fear that the others would misbehave.... Fire, in particular, would want to burn the dead, as of old; and that is no longer done.... I shall leave you alone with Mytyl....

TYLTYL
And may not Tylo stay with us?...

THE DOG
Yes, yes, I shall stay; I shall stay here I... I want to stay with my little god!...

LIGHT
It is impossible.... The Fairy gave formal orders; besides, there is nothing to fear....

THE DOG
Very well, very well, it makes no difference. If they are vicious, my little god, all you have to do Is this ... (he whistles) and you shall see.... It will be just as in the forest: Wow! Wow! Wow!...

LIGHT
Come, good-bye, dear children ... I shall not be far away.... (She kisses the CHILDREN.) Those who love me and whom I love always find me again.... (To the THINGS *and the* ANIMALS) This way, all of

you....

(She goes out with the THINGS *and the* ANIMALS. *The* CHILDREN *remain alone in the middle of the stage. The curtain, opens and*
discloses the next scene.)

SCENE 2.--The Graveyard.

It is night. The moon is shining on a country graveyard.. Numerous tombstones, grassy mounds, wooden crosses, stone slabs, etc. TYLTYL and MYTYL *are standing by a short stone pillar*.

MYTYL
I am frightened!...

TYLTYL (not too much at his ease)
I am never frightened....

MYTYL
I say, are the dead wicked?...

TYLTYL
Why, no, they're not alive!...

MYTYL
Have you ever seen one?...

TYLTYL
Yes, once, long ago, when I was very young....

MYTYL
What was it like, say?...

TYLTYL
Quite white, very still and very cold and it didn't talk....

MYTYL
Are we going to see them, say?...

TYLTYL
Why, of course, Light said so....

MYTYL
Where are they?...

TYLTYL
Here, under the grass or under those big stones....

MYTYL
Are they there all the year round?...

TYLTYL
Yes.

MYTYL (pointing to the slabs)
Are those the doors of their houses?...

TYLTYL
Yes.

MYTYL
Do they go out when it's fine?...

TYLTYL
They can only go out at night....

MYTYL
Why?...

TYLTYL
Because they are in their shirts....

MYTYL
Do they go out also when it rains?...

TYLTYL
When it rains, they stay at home....

MYTYL
Is it nice in their homes, say?...

TYLTYL
They say it's very cramped....

MYTYL
Have they any little children?...

TYLTYL
Why, yes; they have all those that die....

MYTYL
And what do they live on?...

TYLTYL
They eat roots....

MYTYL
Shall we see them?...

TYLTYL
Of course; we see everything when I turn the diamond.

MYTYL
And what will they say?...

TYLTYL
They will say nothing, as they don't talk....

MYTYL
Why don't they talk?...

TYLTYL
Because they have nothing to say....

MYTYL
Why have they nothing to say?...

TYLTYL
You're a nuisance....

(A pause)

MYTYL
When will you turn the diamond?

TYLTYL
You heard Light say that I was to wait until midnight, because that disturbs them less....

MYTYL
Why does that disturb them less?...

TYLTYL
Because that is when they go out to take the air....

MYTYL
Is it not midnight yet?...

TYLTYL
Do you see the church clock?...

MYTYL
Yes, I can even see the small hand....

TYLTYL
Well, midnight is just going to strike.... There!... Do you hear?...

(The clock strikes twelve)

MYTYL
I want to go away!...

TYLTYL
Not now.... I am going to turn the diamond....

MYTYL
No, no!... Don't!... I want to go away!... I am so frightened, little brother!... I am terribly frightened!...

TYLTYL
But there is no danger....

MYTYL
I don't want to see the dead!... I don't want to see them!...

TYLTYL
Very well, you shall not see them; shut your eyes....

MYTYL (clinging to TYLTYL'S *clothes*)
Tyltyl, I can't stay!... No, I can't possibly!... They are going to come out of the ground!...

TYLTYL
Don't tremble like that.... They will only come out for a moment....

MYTYL
But you're trembling, too!... They will be awful!...

TYLTYL
It is time, the hour is passing....

(TYLTYL *turns the diamond. A terrifying minute of silence and motionlessness elapses, after which, slowly, the crosses totter, the mounds open, the slabs rise up....*)

MYTYL (cowering against TYLTYL)
They are coming out!... They are there!...

(Then, from all the gaping tombs, there rises gradually an efflorescence at first frail and timid, like steam; then white and virginal and more and more tufty, more and more tall and plentiful and marvellous. Little by little, irresistibly, invading all things, it transforms the graveyard into a sort of fairy-like and nuptial garden, over which rise the first rays of the dawn. The dew glitters, the flowers open their blooms, the wind murmurs in the leaves, the bees hum, the birds wake and flood the air with the first raptures of their hymns to the sun and to life. Stunned and dazzled, TYLTYL *and* MYTYL, *holding each other by the hand, take a few steps among the flowers while they seek for the trace of the tombs*.)

MYTYL (looking in the grass)
Where are the dead?....

TYLTYL (looking also)
There are no dead....

CURTAIN

SCENE 3.--The Kingdom of the Future.

The immense halls of the Azure Palace, where the children wait that are yet to be born. Infinite perspectives of sapphire columns supporting turquoise vaults. Everything, from the light and the lapis-lazuli flagstones to the shimmering background into which the last arches run and disappear, everything, down to the smallest objects, is of an unreal, intense, fairy-like blue. Only the plinths and capitals of the columns, the key-stones, a few seats and circular benches are of white marble or alabaster. To the right, between the columns, are great opalescent doors. These doors, which TIME *will throw back towards the end of the*

scene, open upon actual life and the quays of the Dawn. Everywhere, harmoniously peopling the hall, is a crowd of CHILDREN *robed in long azure garments. Some are playing, others strolling to and fro, others talking or dreaming; many are asleep, many also are working, between the colonnades, at future inventions; and their tools, their instruments, the apparatus which they are constructing, the plants, flowers and fruit which they are cultivating or plucking are of the same supernatural and luminous*
blue *as the general atmosphere of the Palace. Figures of a taller stature, clad in a paler and more diaphanous azure, figures of a sovereign and silent beauty move among the* CHILDREN *and would seem to be angels.*

Enter on the left, as though by stealth, gliding between the columns in the foreground, TYLTYL, MYTYL *and* LIGHT. *Their arrival causes* a certain movement among the BLUE CHILDREN, *who come running up on every hand, form a group around the unwonted visitors and gaze upon them*
with curiosity.

MYTYL
Where are Sugar, the Cat and Bread?...

LIGHT
They cannot enter here; they would know the future and would not obey....

TYLTYL
And the Dog?...

LIGHT
It is not well, either, that he should know what awaits him in the course of the ages....I have locked them all up in the vaults of the church....

TYLTYL
Where are we?...

LIGHT
We are in the Kingdom of the Future, in the midst of the children who are not yet born. As the diamond allows us to see clearly in this region which is hidden from men, we shall very probably find the Blue Bird here....

TYLTYL
Certainly the bird will be blue, since everything here is blue....(Looking all around him.) Heaven, how beautiful it all is!...

LIGHT
Look at the children running up....

TYLTYL
Are they angry?...

LIGHT
Not at all....You can see, they are smiling, but they are surprised....

THE BLUE CHILDREN (running up in ever-increasing numbers)
Live children!...Come and look at the little live children!...

TYLTYL
Why do they call us the little live children?

LIGHT
Because they themselves are not alive yet....

TYLTYL
What are they doing, then?...

LIGHT
They are awaiting the hour of their birth....

TYLTYL
The hour of their birth?...

LIGHT
Yes; it is from here that all the children come who are born upon our earth. Each awaits his day.... When the fathers and mothers want children, the great doors which you see there, on the right, are opened and the little ones go down....

TYLTYL
What a, lot there are! What a lot there are!...

LIGHT
There are many more.... We do not see them all.... There are thirty thousand halls like this, all full of them.... Just think, there are enough to last to the end of the world!... No one could count them....

TYLTYL
And those tall blue persons, who are they?...

LIGHT
No one exactly knows.... They are believed to be guardians.... I have heard that they will come upon earth after men.... But we are not allowed to ask them....

TYLTYL
Why not?...

LIGHT
Because it is the earth's secret....

TYLTYL
And may one talk to the others, the little ones?...

LIGHT
Certainly; you must make friends.... Look, there is one who is more curious than the rest.... Go up to him, speak to him....

TYLTYL
What shall I say to him?...

LIGHT
Whatever you like, as you would to a little playfellow....

TYLTYL
Can I shake hands with him?...

LIGHT
Of course, he won't hurt you.... But come, don't look so constrained.... I will leave you alone, you will be more at ease by yourselves.... Besides, I want to speak to the tall blue person....

TYLTYL (going up to the BLUE CHILD *and holding out his hand*)
How do you do?... (Touching the CHILD'S *blue dress with his finger*.) What's that?...

THE CHILD (gravely touching TYLTYL'S *hat*)
And that?...

TYLTYL
That?... That is my hat.... Have you no hat?...

THE CHILD
No; what is it for?...

TYLTYL
It's to say How-do-you-do with.... And then for when it rains or when it's cold....

THE CHILD
What does that mean, when it's cold?...

TYLTYL
When you shiver like this: brrrr! brrrr!... When you blow into your hands and go like this with your arms....

(He vigorously beats his arms across his chest.)

THE CHILD
Is it cold on earth?...

TYLTYL
Yes, sometimes, in the winter, when there is no fire....

THE CHILD
Why is there no fire?...

TYLTYL
Because it's expensive and it costs money to buy wood....

THE CHILD
What is money?...

TYLTYL
It's what you pay with....

THE CHILD
Oh....

TYLTYL
Some people have money and others have none....

THE CHILD
Why not?...

TYLTYL
Because they are not rich.... Are you rich?... How old are you?...

THE CHILD
I am going to be born soon.... I shall be born in twelve years.... Is it nice to be born?...

TYLTYL
Oh, yes!... It's great fun!...

THE CHILD
How did you manage?...

TYLTYL
I can't remember.... It is so long ago!...

THE CHILD
They say it's lovely, the earth and the live people!...

TYLTYL
Yes, it's not bad.... There are birds and cakes and toys.... Some have them all; but those who have none can look at them....

THE CHILD
They tell us that the mothers stand waiting at the door.... They are good, aren't they?...

TYLTYL
Oh, yes!... They are better than anything in the world!... And the grannies too; but they die too soon....

THE CHILD
They die?... What is that?...

TYLTYL
They go away one evening and do not come back....

THE CHILD
Why?...

TYLTYL
How can one tell?... Perhaps because they feel sad....

THE CHILD
Has yours gone?...

TYLTYL
My grandmamma?...

THE CHILD
Your mamma or your grandmamma, I don't know....

TYLTYL
Oh, but it's not the same thing!... The grannies go first; that's sad enough.... Mine was very kind to me....

THE CHILD
What is the matter with your eyes?.... Are they making pearls?...

TYLTYL
No; it's not pearls....

THE CHILD
What is it, then?...

TYLTYL
It's nothing; it's all that blue, which dazzles me a little....

THE CHILD
What is that called?...

TYLTYL
What?...

THE CHILD
There, that, falling down....

TYLTYL
Nothing, it is a little water....

THE CHILD
Does it come from the eyes?...

TYLTYL
Yes, sometimes, when one cries....

THE CHILD
What does that mean, crying?...

TYLTYL
I have not been crying; it is the fault of that blue... But if I had cried, it would be the same thing....

THE CHILD
Does one often cry?...

TYLTYL
Not little boys, but little girls do.... Don't you cry here?...

THE CHILD
No; I don't know how....

TYLTYL
Well, you will learn.... What are you playing with, those great blue wings?...

THE CHILD
These?... That's for the invention which I shall make on earth....

TYLTYL
What invention?... Have you invented something?...

THE CHILD
Why, yes; haven't you heard?... When I am on earth, I shall have to invent the thing that gives happiness....

TYLTYL
Is it good to eat?... Does it make a noise?...

THE CHILD
No; you hear nothing....

TYLTYL
That's a pity....

THE CHILD
I work at it every day.... It is almost finished.... Would you like to see it?...

TYLTYL
Very much.... Where is it?...

THE CHILD
There, you can see it from here, between those two columns....

ANOTHER BLUE CHILD (coming up to TYLTYL *and plucking his sleeve*)
Would you like to see mine, say?...

TYLTYL
Yes, what is it?...

THE SECOND CHILD
The thirty-three remedies for prolonging life.... There, in those blue phials....

A THIRD CHILD (stepping out from the crowd)
I will show you a light which nobody knows of!... (He lights himself up entirely with an extraordinary flame.) It's rather curious, isn't it?...

A FOURTH CHILD (pulling TYLTYL'S *arm*)
Do come and look at my machine which flies in the air like a bird without wings!...

A FIFTH CHILD
No, no; mine first! It discovers the treasures hidden in the moon!...

THE BLUE CHILDREN (crowding round TYLTYL *and* MYTYL *and all cry-*

ing together)
No, no, come and see mine!... No, mine is much finer!... Mine is a wonderful invention!... Mine is made of sugar!... His is no good!... He stole the idea from me!...

(*Amid these disordered exclamations, the* LIVE CHILDREN *are dragged towards the blue workshops, where each of the inventors sets his ideal machine going. There ensues a cerulean whirl of wheels, disks, flywheels, driving-wheels, pulleys, straps and strange and as yet unnamed objects shrouded in the bluey mists of the unreal. A crowd of odd and mysterious mechanisms dart forth and hover under the vaults or crawl at the foot of the columns, while* CHILDREN *unfold charts and plans, open books, uncover azure statues and bring enormous flowers and gigantic fruits that seem formed of sapphires and turquoises.*)

A LITTLE BLUE CHILD (bending under the weight of some colossal blue daisies)
Look at my flowers!...

TYLTYL
What are they?... I don't know them....

THE LITTLE BLUE CHILD
They are daisies!...

TYLTYL
Impossible!... They are as big as tables!...

THE LITTLE BLUE CHILD
And they smell so good!...

TYLTYL (smelling them)
Wonderful!...

THE LITTLE BLUE CHILD
They will grow like that when I am on earth....

TYLTYL
When will that be?...

THE LITTLE BLUE CHILD
In fifty-three years, four months and nine days....

(Two BLUE CHILDREN *arrive, carrying, like a lustre hanging on a pole, an incredible bunch of grapes, each larger than a pear*.)

ONE OF THE CHILDREN (carrying the grapes)
What do you say to my fruits?...

TYLTYL
A bunch of pears!...

THE CHILD
No, they are grapes!... They will all be like that when I am thirty.... I have found the way....

ANOTHER CHILD (staggering under a basket of blue apples the size of melons)
And mine!... Look at my apples!...

TYLTYL
But those are melons!...

THE CHILD
No, no!... They are my apples and they are not the finest at that!... They will all be alike when I am alive.... I have discovered the system!...

ANOTHER CHILD (wheeling a blue barrow with blue melons bigger than pumpkins)
What do you say to my little melons?...

TYLTYL
But they are pumpkins!...

THE CHILD WITH THE MELONS
When I come on earth, the melons will be splendid!... I shall be the gardener of the King of the Three Planets....

TYLTYL
The King of the Three Planets?

THE CHILD WITH THE MELONS
The great king who for thirty-five years will bring happiness to the Earth, Mars and the Moon.... You can see him from here....

TYLTYL
Where is he?...

THE CHILD WITH THE MELONS
There, the little boy sleeping at the foot of that column.

TYLTYL
On the left?...

THE CHILD WITH THE MELONS
No, on the right.... The one on the left is the child who will bring pure

joy to the globe....

TYLTYL
How?...

THE CHILD (the one that first talked to TYLTYL)
By means of ideas which people have not yet had....

TYLTYL
And the other, that little fat one with his fingers to his nose, what will he do?...

THE CHILD
He is to discover the fire that will warm the earth when the sun is paler than now....

TYLTYL
And the two holding each other by the hand and always kissing; are they brother and sister?...

THE CHILD
No; they are very comical....They are the Lovers....

TYLTYL
What is that?...

THE CHILD
I don't know.... Time calls them that, to make fun of them.... They spend the day looking into each other's eyes, kissing and bidding each other farewell....

TYLTYL
Why?...

THE CHILD
It seems that they will not be able to leave together....

TYLTYL
And the little pink one, who looks so serious and is sucking his thumb, what is he?...

THE CHILD
It appears that he is to wipe out injustice from the earth....

TYLTYL
Oh!...

THE CHILD
They say it's a tremendous work....

TYLTYL
And the little red-haired one, who walks as if he did not see where he was going, is he blind?...

THE CHILD
Not yet; but he will become so....Look at him well; it seems that he is to conquer Death....

TYLTYL
What does that mean?...

THE CHILD
I don't exactly know; but they say it's a great thing....

TYLTYL (pointing to a crowd of CHILDREN *sleeping at the foot of the columns, on the steps, the benches, etc.*)
And all those asleep, what a number of them there are asleep!... Do they do

nothing?...

THE CHILD
They are thinking of something....

TYLTYL
Of what?...

THE CHILD
They do not know yet; but they must take something with them to earth; we are not allowed to go from here empty-handed....

TYLTYL
Who says so?...

THE CHILD
Time, who stands at the door.... You will see when he opens it.... He is very tiresome....

A CHILD (running up from the back of the hall and elbowing his way through the crowd)
How are you, TYLTYL?...

TYLTYL
Hullo!... How does he know my name?...

THE CHILD (who has just run up and who now kisses TYLTYL *and* MYTYL *effusively*.)
How are you?... All right?... Come, give me a kiss, and you too, Mytyl. It's not surprising that I should know your name, seeing that I shall be your brother.... They have only just told me that you were here.... I was right at the other end of the hall, packing up my ideas.... Tell mummy that I am ready....

TYLTYL
What?... Are you coming to us?...

THE CHILD
Certainly, next year, on Palm Sunday.... Don't tease me too much when I am little.... I am very glad to have kissed you both beforehand.... Tell daddy to mend the cradle.... Is it comfortable in our home?...

TYLTYL
Not bad.... And mummy is so kind!...

THE CHILD
And the food?...

TYLTYL
That depends.... We even have cakes sometimes, don't we, Mytyl?...

MYTYL
On New Year's Day and the fourteenth of July.... Mummy makes them....

TYLTYL
What have you got in that bag?... Are you bringing us something?...

THE CHILD
I am bringing three illnesses: scarlatina, whooping-cough and measles....

TYLTYL
Oh, that's all, is it?... And, after that, what will you do?...

THE CHILD
After that?... I shall leave you....

TYLTYL
It will hardly be worth while coming!...

THE CHILD
We can't pick and choose!...

(At that moment, a sort of prolonged, powerful, crystalline vibration is heard to rise and swell; it seems to emanate from the columns and the opal doors, which are irradiated by a brighter light than before.)

TYLTYL
What is that?...

THE CHILD
That's Time!... He is going to open the gates!...

(A great change comes over the crowd of BLUE CHILDREN, *Most of them leave their machines and their labours, numbers of sleepers awake and*
all turn their eyes towards the opal doors and go nearer to them.)

LIGHT (joining TYLTYL)
Let us try to hide behind the columns.... It will not do for Time to discover us....

TYLTYL
Where does that noise come from?...

A CHILD
It is the Dawn rising.... This is the hour when the children who are to be born to-day go down to earth....

TYLTYL
How will they go down?... Are there ladders?...

THE CHILD
You shall see.... Time is drawing the bolts....

TYLTYL
Who is Time?...

THE CHILD
An old man who comes to call those who are going....

TYLTYL
Is he wicked?...

THE CHILD
No; but he hears nothing.... Beg as they may, if it's not their turn, he pushes back all those who try to go....

TYLTYL
Are they glad to go?...

THE CHILD
We are sorry when we are left behind, but we are sad when we go.... There! There!... He is opening the doors!...

(The great opalescent doors turn slowly on their hinges. The sounds of the earth are heard like a distant music. A red and green light penetrates into the hall; TIME, *a tall old man with a streaming beard, armed with his scythe and hourglass, appears upon the threshold; and the spectator perceives the extremity of the white and gold sails of a galley moored to a sort of quay, formed by the rosy mists of the Dawn*.)

TIME (on the threshold)
Are they ready whose hour has struck?...

BLUE CHILDREN (elbowing their way and running up from all sides)
Here we are!... Here we are!... Here we are!...

TIME (in a gruff voice to the CHILDREN *defiling before him to go out*)
One at a time!... Once again, there are many more of you than are wanted!... It's always the same thing!... You can't deceive me!...(Pushing back a CHILD.) It's not your turn!... Go back and wait till to-morrow.... Nor you either; go in and return in ten years.... A thirteenth shepherd?... There are only twelve wanted; there is no need for more; the days of Theocritus and Virgil are past.... More doctors?... There are too many already; they are grumbling about it on earth.... And where are the engineers?... They want an honest man, only one, as a phenomenon.... Where is the honest man?... Is it you?... (THE CHILD *nods yes*.) You appear to me to be a very poor specimen!... Hallo, you, over there, not so fast, not so fast!... And you, what are you bringing?... Nothing at all, empty-handed?... Then you can't go through.... Prepare something, a great crime, if you like, or a fine sickness, I don't care ... but you mast have something.... (Catching sight of a little CHILD whom the others are pushing forward, while he resists with all his strength.) Well, what's the matter with you?... You know that the hour has come.... They want a hero to fight against injustice; you're the one: you most start....

THE BLUE CHILDREN
He doesn't want to, sir....

TIME
What?... He doesn't want to?... Where does the little monster think he is?... No objections, we have no time to spare....

THE CHILD (who is being pushed)
No, no!...I don't want to go!... I would rather not be born!... I would rather stay here!...

TIME
That is not the question.... When the hour comes, it comes!... Now then, quick, forward!...

A CHILD (stepping forward)
Oh, let me pass!... I will go and take his place!... They say that my parents are old and have been waiting for me so long!...

TIME
None of that!... You will start at your proper hour, at your proper time.... We should never be done if we listened to you.... One wants to go, another refuses; it's too soon or it's too late.... (Pushing back some CHILDREN *who have encroached upon the threshold*.) Not so near, you children!... Back, you inquisitive ones!... Those who are not starting have no business outside.... You are in a hurry now; later, when your turn comes, you will be frightened and hang back.... Look, there are four who are trembling like leaves.... (To a CHILD *who, on the point of crossing the threshold, suddenly goes back*.) Well, what is it?... What's the matter?...

THE CHILD
I have forgotten the box containing the two crimes which I shall have to commit....

ANOTHER CHILD
And I the little pot with my idea for enlightening the crowd....

A THIRD CHILD
I have forgotten the graft of my finest pear!...

TIME
Run quick and fetch them!... We have only six hundred and twelve seconds left.... The galley of the Dawn is already flapping her sails to show that she is waiting.... You will come too late and you won't be born!... Come, quick, on board with you!... (Laying hold of a CHILD *who tries to pass between his legs to reach the quay*.) Oh, no, not you!... This is the third time you've tried to be born before your turn.... Don't let me catch you at it again, or you can wait forever with my sister Eternity; and you know that it's not amusing there!... But come, are we ready?... Is every one at his post?... (Surveying the CHILDREN *standing on the quay or already seated In the galley*.) There is still one missing.... It is no use his hiding, I see him in the crowd.... You can't deceive me!... Come on, you, the little fellow whom they call the Lover, say good-bye to your sweetheart....

(*The two* CHILDREN *who are called the Lovers, fondly entwined, their faces livid with despair, go up to* TIME *and kneel at his feet*.)

THE FIRST CHILD
Mr. Time, let me stay behind with her!...

THE SECOND CHILD
Mr. Time, let me go with him!...

TIME
Impossible!... We have only three hundred and ninety-four seconds left....

THE FIRST CHILD
I would rather not be born!...

TIME
You cannot choose....

THE SECOND CHILD (beseechingly)
Mr. Time, I shall come too late!...

THE FIRST CHILD
I shall be gone before she comes down!...

THE SECOND CHILD
I shall never see him again!...

THE FIRST CHILD
We shall be alone in the world!...

TIME
All this does not concern me.... Address your entreaties to Life.... I unite and part as I am told....(Seizing one of the CHILDREN.) Come!...

THE FIRST CHILD (struggling)
No, no, no!... She, too!...

THE SECOND CHILD (clinging to the clothes of the FIRST)
Leave him with me!... Leave him!...

TIME
Come, come, he is not going to die, but to live!... (Dragging away the FIRST CHILD.) Come along!...

THE SECOND CHILD (stretching her arms out frantically to the CHILD that is being carried off)
A sign!... A sign!... Tell me how to find you!...

THE FIRST CHILD
I shall always love you!...

THE SECOND CHILD
I shall be the saddest thing on earth!... You will know me by that!...

(She falls and remains stretched on the ground.)

TIME
You would do much better to hope.... And now, that is all....
(Consulting his hour-glass.) We have only sixty-three seconds left....

(Last and violent movements among the CHILDREN *departing and remaining. They exchange hurried farewells*.)

THE BLUE CHILDREN
Good-bye, Pierre!... Good-bye, Jean!... Have you all you want?... Announce my idea!... Have you got the new turnscrew?... Mind you speak of my melons!... Have you forgotten nothing?... Try to know me again I... I shall find you!... Don't lose your ideas!... Don't lean too far into space!... Send me your news!... They say one can't... Oh, try, do try!... Try to tell us if it's nice!... I will come to meet you I... I shall be born on a throne!...

TIME (shaking his keys and his scythe)
Enough! Enough!... The anchor's raised!...

(The sails of the galley pass and disappear. The voices of the CHILDREN *in the galley are heard in the distance*: "The Earth! The Earth!... I can see it!... How beautiful it is!... How bright it is!... How big it is!"... *Then, as though issuing from the depths of the abyss, an extremely distant song of gladness and expectation*.)

TYLTYL (to LIGHT)
What is that?... It is not they singing.... It sounds like other voices....

LIGHT
Yes, it is the song of the mothers coming out to meet them....

(Meanwhile, TIME *closes the opalescent doors. He turns to take a last look at the hall and suddenly perceives* TYLTYL, MYTYL and LIGHT.)

TIME (dumbfounded and furious)
What's that?... What are you doing here?... Who are you?... Why are you not blue?... How did you get in?... (He comes forward, threatening them with his scythe.)

LIGHT (to TYLTYL)
Do not answer!... I have the Blue Bird.... He is hidden under my cloak.... Let us escape.... Turn the diamond, he will lose our traces.... (They slip away on the left, between the columns in the foreground.)

CURTAIN

ACT VI

SCENE I.--The Leave-taking.

The stage represents a wall with a small door. It is the break of day.

(Enter TYLTYL, MYTYL, LIGHT, BREAD, WATER, SUGAR, FIRE *and* MILK) You would never guess where we are....

TYLTYL
Well, no, Light, because I don't know....

LIGHT
Don't you recognise that wall and that little door?...

TYLTYL
It is a red wall and a little green door.

LIGHT
And doesn't that remind you of anything?...

TYLTYL
It reminds me that Time shewed us the door....

LIGHT
How odd people are when they dream.... They do not recognise their own hands....

TYLTYL
Who is dreaming?... Am I?...

LIGHT
Perhaps it's myself.... Who can tell?... However, this wall contains a house which you have seen more than once since you were born....

TYLTYL
A house which I have seen more than once since I was born?...

LIGHT
Why yes, sleepy-head!... It is the house which we left one evening, just a year ago, to a day....

TYLTYL
Just a year ago?... Why, then....

LIGHT
Come, come!... Don't open great eyes like sapphire caves.... It's the dear old house of your father and mother....

TYLTYL (going up to the door)
But I think.... Yes, really.... It seems to me.... This little door.... I recognise the wooden pin.... Are they in there?... Are we near mummy?... I want to go in at once.... I want to kiss her at once!...

LIGHT
One moment.... They are sound asleep; you must not wake them with a start.... Besides, the door will not open till the hour strikes....

TYLTYL
What hour?... Is there long to wait?...

LIGHT
Alas, no!... A few poor minutes....

TYLTYL
Aren't you glad to be back?... What is it, Light?... You are quite pale, you look ill....

LIGHT
It's nothing, child.... I feel a little sad, because I am leaving you....

TYLTYL
Leaving us?...

LIGHT
I must.... I have nothing more to do here; the year is over, the Fairy is coming back to ask you for the Blue Bird....

TYLTYL
But I haven't got the Blue Bird!... The one of the Land of Memory turned quite black, the one of the Future turned quite pink, the Night's are dead and I could not catch the one in the Forest.... Is it my fault if they change colour, or die, or escape?... Will the Fairy be angry and what will she say?...

LIGHT
We have done what we could.... It seems likely that the Blue Bird does not exist or that he changes colour when he is caged....

TYLTYL
Where is the cage?...

BREAD
Here, master.... It was entrusted to my diligent care during our long journey; to-day, now that my mission is drawing to an end, I restore it to your hands, untouched and carefully closed, as I received it.... (Like an orator making a speech) And now, in the name of all, I crave permission to add a few words....

FIRE
He has not been called upon to speak!...

WATER
Order!...

BREAD
The malevolent interruptions of a contemptible enemy, of an envious rival....

FIRE
An envious rival!... What would you be without me?... A lump of shapeless and indigestible dough....

WATER
Order!...

FIRE
I won't be shouted down by you! ...

(They threaten each other and are about to come to blows.)

LIGHT (raising her wand)
Enough!...

BREAD
The insults and the ridiculous pretensions of an element whose notorious misbehaviour and whose scandalous excesses drive the world to despair....

FIRE
You fat pasty-face!

BREAD (raising his voice)
Will not prevent me from doing my duty to the end.... I wish, therefore, in the name of all...

FIRE
Not in mine!... I have a tongue of my own!...

BREAD
In the name of all and with a restrained but simple and deep emotion, to take leave of two distinguished children, whose exalted mission ends to-day.... When bidding them farewell, with all the grief and all the fondness which a mutual esteem....

TYLTYL
What?... You are bidding us farewell?... Are you leaving us too?...

BREAD
Alas, needs must, since the hour when men's eyes are to be opened has not yet come.... I am leaving you, it is true; but the separation will only be apparent, you will no longer hear me speak....

FIRE
That will be no loss!...

WATER
Order! Silence!...

FIRE
I shall keep silence when you cease babbling in the kettles, the wells, the brooks, the waterfalls and the taps....

LIGHT (threatening them with her wand)
That will do, do you hear?... You are all very quarrelsome; It is the coming separation that sets your nerves on edge like this....

BREAD (with great dignity)
That does not apply to me.... I was saying, you will no longer hear me speak, no longer see me in my living form.... Your eyes are about to close to the invisible life of the Things; but I shall always he there. In the bread-pan, on the shelf, on the table, beside the soup, I who am, if I may say so, with Water and Fire, the most faithful companion, the oldest friend of Man....

FIRE
Well, and what about me?...

LIGHT
Come, the minutes are passing, the hour is at hand which will send us back into silence.... Be quick and kiss the children....

FIRE (rushing forward)
I first! I first!... (Violently kissing the CHILDREN.) Good-bye, Tyltyl and Mytyl!... Good-bye, my darlings.... Think of me if ever you want any one to set fire to anything....

MYTYL
Oh! Oh!... He's burning me!...

TYLTYL
Oh! Oh!... He's scorched my nose!...

LIGHT
Come, Fire, moderate your transports.... Remember you're not in your chimney....

WATER
What an idiot!...

BREAD
What a vulgarian!...

FIRE
There, look; I will put my hands in my pockets.... But don't forget me.... I am the friend of Man.... I shall always be there, in the hearth and in the oven; and I will come sometimes and put out my tongue for you when you are cold or sad.... I shall be warm in winter and roast chestnuts for you....

WATER (approaching the CHILDREN)
I shall kiss you without hurting you, tenderly, my children....

FIRE
Take care, you'll get wet!...

WATER
I am loving and gentle; I am kind to human beings....

FIRE
What about those you drown?...

WATER
Love the wells, listen to the brooks.... I shall always be there....

FIRE
She has flooded the whole place....

WATER
When you sit down, in the evening, beside the springs--there is more than one here in the forest--try to understand what they are trying to say....

FIRE
Enough! Enough!... I can't swim!...

WATER
I shall no longer be able to tell you as clearly as I do to-day that I love you; but you will not forget that that is what I am saying to you when you hear my voice.... Alas!... I can say no more.... My tears choke me and prevent my speaking....

FIRE
It doesn't sound like it!...

WATER
Think of me when you see the water-bottle.... Alas! I have to be silent there; but my thoughts will always be of you.... You will find me also in the ewer, the watering-can, the cistern and the tap....

MILK (approaching timidly)
And me in the milk-jug....

TYLTYL
What, you too, my dear Milk, so shy and so good?... Is everybody going?...

SUGAR (naturally mawkish and sanctimonious)
If you have a little corner left in your memory, remember sometimes that my presence was sweet to you.... That is all I have to say.... Tears are not

in harmony with my temperament and they hurt me terribly when they fall on
my feet....

BREAD
Jesuit!...

FIRE (yelping)
Sugar-plum! Lollipop! Caramel!...

TYLTYL
But where are Tylette and Tylo gone to?... What are they doing?...

(The CAT *is heard to utter shrill cries*.)

MYTYL (alarmed)
It's Tylette crying!... He is being hurt!...

(Enter the CAT, *running, his hair on end and dishevelled, his clothes torn, holding his handkerchief to his cheek, as though he had the toothache. He utters angry groans and is closely pursued by the* DOG, who overwhelms him with bites, blows and kicks.)

THE DOG (beating the CAT)
There!... Have you had enough?... Do you want any more?... There! There! There!...

LIGHT, TYLTYL and MYTYL (rushing forward to part them)
Tylo!... Are you mad?... Well, I never!... Down!... Stop that, will you?... How dare you?... Wait, wait!...

(They part the DOG *and the* CAT *by main force*.)

LIGHT
What is it?... What has happened?...

THE CAT (blubbering and wiping his eyes)
It's the Dog, Mrs. Light.... He insulted me, he put tin tacks in my food, he pulled my tail, he beat me; and I had done nothing, nothing, nothing at all!...

THE DOG (mimicking him)
Nothing, nothing, nothing at all!... (In an undertone, with a mocking grimace) Never mind, you've had some, you've had some and you're going to have some more!...

MYTYL (pressing the CAT *in her arms*)
My poor Tylette, where has he hurt you?... Tell me.... I shall cry too....

LIGHT (to the DOG, *severely*)
Your conduct is all the more, unworthy since you have chosen for this disgraceful exhibition the already most painful moment when we are about to part from these poor children....

THE DOG (suddenly sobered)
To part from these poor children?...

LIGHT
Yes; the hour which you know of is at hand.... We are going to return to silence.... We shall no longer be able to speak to them....

THE DOG (suddenly uttering real howls of despair and flinging himself upon the CHILDREN, *whom he loads with violent and tumultuous caresses*.)
No! No!... I refuse!... I refuse!... I shall always talk!... You will

understand me now, will you not, my little god?... Yes! Yes! Yes!... And we shall tell each other everything, everything, everything!... And I shall be very good.... And I shall learn to read and write and play dominoes!... And I shall always be very clean.... And I shall never steal anything in the kitchen again.... Shall I do a wonderful trick for you?... Would you like me to kiss the Cat?...

MYTYL (to the CAT)
And you, Tylette?... Have you nothing to say to us?...

THE CAT (in an affected and enigmatic tone)
I love you both as much as you deserve....

LIGHT
Now let me, in my turn, children, give you a last kiss....

TYLTYL and MYTYL (hanging on to LIGHT'S *dress*)
No, no, no, Light!... Stay here with us!... Daddy won't mind.... We will tell mummy how kind you have been....

LIGHT
Alas! I cannot!... This door is closed to us and I must leave you....

TYLTYL
Where will you go all alone?...

LIGHT
Not very far, my children; over there, to the Land of the Silence of Things....

TYLTYL
No, no; I won't have you go.... We will go with you.... I shall tell mummy....

LIGHT

Do not cry, my dear little ones.... I have not a voice like Water; I have only my brightness, which Man does not understand.... But I watch over him to the end of his days.... Never forget that I am speaking to you in every spreading moonbeam, in every twinkling star, in every dawn that rises, in every lamp that is lit, in every good and bright thought of your soul.... (Eight o'clock strikes behind the wall.) Listen!... The hour is striking!... Good-bye!... The door is opening!... In with you, in with you!...

(She pushes the CHILDREN *through the door, which has half-opened and which closes again behind them*. BREAD *wipes away a furtive tear*, SUGAR *and* WATER, *etc., all in tears, flee precipitously and disappear in the wings to the right and left. The* DOG *howls behind the scenes. The stage remains empty for a moment and then the scenery representing the wall and the little door opens in the middle and reveals the last scene*.)

SCENE 2.--The Awakening.

The same setting as in ACT I, *but the objects, the walls and the atmosphere all appear incomparably and magically fresher, happier, more smiling. The daylight penetrates gaily through the chinks of the closed shutters. To the right, at the back*, TYLTYL *and* MYTYL *lie sound asleep in their little beds. The* DOG, *the* CAT *and the* THINGS *are in the places which they occupied in* ACT I, before the arrival of the FAIRY.

Enter MUMMY TYL

MUMMY TYL (in a cheerfully scolding voice)
Up, come, get up, you little lazybones!... Aren't you ashamed of yourselves?... It has struck eight and the sun is high above the trees!... Lord, how they sleep, how they sleep!... (She leans over and kisses the CHILDREN.) They are quite rosy.... Tyltyl smells of lavender and Mytyl of lilies-of-the-valley.... (Kissing them again) What sweet things children are!... Still, they can't go on sleeping till midday.... I mustn't let them grow up idle.... And, besides, I have heard that it's not very healthy.... (Gently shaking TYLTYL) Wake up, wake up, Tyltyl....

TYLTYL (waking up)
What?... Light?... Where is she?... No, no, don't go away....

MUMMY TYL
Light?... Why, of course it's light... Has been for ever so long.... It's as bright as noonday, though the shutters are closed.... Wait a bit till I open them.... (She pushes back the shutters and the dazzling daylight

invades the room.) There! See!... What's the matter with you?... You look quite blinded....

TYLTYL (rubbing his eyes)
Mummy, mummy!... It's you!...

MUMMY TYL
Why, of course, it's I.... Who did you think it was?...

TYLTYL
It's you.... Yes, yes, it's you!....

MUMMY TYL
Yes, yes, it's I.... I haven't changed my face since last night.... Why do you stare at me in that wonderstruck way?... Is my nose turned upside down, by any chance?...

TYLTYL
Oh, how nice it is to see you again!... It's so long, so long ago!... I must kiss you at once.... Again! Again! Again!... And how comfortable my bed is!... I am back at home!...

MUMMY TYL
What's the matter?... Why don't you wake up?... Don't tell me you're ill.... Let me see, show me your tongue.... Come, get up and dress....

TYLTYL
Hullo, I've got my shirt on!...

MUMMY TYL
Of course you have.... Put on your breeches and your little jacket.... There they are, on the chair....

TYLTYL
Is that what I did on the journey?...

MUMMY TYL
What journey?...

TYLTYL
Why, last year....

MUMMY TYL
Last year?...

TYLTYL
Why, yes!...At Christmas, when I went away....

MUMMY TYL
When you went away?... You haven't left the room.... I put you to bed last night, and here you are this morning.... Have you dreamed all that?...

TYLTYL
But you don't understand!... It was last year, when I went away with Mytyl, the Fairy, Light--how nice Light is!--Bread, Sugar, Water, Fire: they did nothing but quarrel!... You're not angry with me?... Did you feel very sad?... And what did daddy say?... I could not refuse... I left a note to explain....

MUMMY TYL
What are you talking about?... For sure, either you're ill or else you're still asleep.... (She gives him a friendly shake.) There, wake up.... There, is that better?...

TYLTYL
But, mummy, I assure you.... It's you that's still asleep....

MUMMY TYL
What! Still asleep, am I?... Why? I've been up since six o'clock.... I've finished all the cleaning and lit the fire....

TYLTYL
But ask Mytyl if it's not true.... Oh, we have had such adventures!...

MUMMY TYL
Why Mytyl?... What do you mean?...

TYLTYL
She was with me.... We saw grandad and granny....

MUMMY TYL (more and more bewildered)
Grandad and granny?...

TYLTYL
Yes, in the Land of Memory.... It was on our way.... They are dead, but they are quite well.... Granny made us a lovely plum-tart.... And then the little brothers--Robert, Jean and his top--and Madeleine and Pierrette and Pauline and Riquette, too....

MYTYL
Riquette still goes about on all fours!...

TYLTYL
And Pauline still has a pimple on her nose....

MUMMY TYL
Have you found the key of the cupboard where daddy hides his brandy bottle?...

TYLTYL
Does daddy hide a brandy bottle?...

MUMMY TYL
Certainly. One has to hide everything when one has little meddlesome good-for-nothings like you.... But come, out with it, confess that you took it.... I would rather it was that.... I sha'n't tell daddy.... I sha'n't beat you....

TYLTYL
But, mummy, I don't know where it is....

MUMMY TYL
Just walk in front of me, so that I may see if you can walk straight.... (TYLTYL *does so*) No, it's not that.... Dear heaven, what is the matter with them?... I shall lose them too, as I lost the others!... (Suddenly mad with alarm, she calls out) Daddy Tyl!... Come, quick! The children are ill!...

(Enter DADDY TYL, *very calmly, with an axe in his hand*.)

DADDY TYL
What is it?...

TYLTYL and MYTYL (running up gaily to kiss their father)
Hullo, daddy!... It's daddy!... Good-morning, daddy!... Have you had plenty of work this year?...

DADDY TYL
Well, what's the matter?... They don't look ill; they look very well....

MUMMY TYL (weeping)
You can't trust their looks.... It will be as with the others.... They

looked quite well also to the end; and then God took them.... I don't know what's the matter with them.... I put them to bed quite quietly last night; and this morning, when they woke up, everything was wrong.... They don't know what they're saying; they talk about a journey.... They have seen Light and grandad and granny, who are dead, but who are quite well....

TYLTYL
But grandad still has his wooden leg....

MYTYL
And granny her rheumatics....

MUMMY TYL
Do you hear?... Run and fetch the doctor!...

DADDY TYL
Why, no, no.... They are not dead yet.... Come, let us look into this....
(A knock at the front door.) Come in!...

(Enter NEIGHBOUR BERLINGOT, *a little old woman resembling the* FAIRY *in* ACT I *and leaning on a stick*.)

THE NEIGHBOUR
Good-morning and a Merry Christmas to you all!...

TYLTYL
It's the Fairy Berylune!...

THE NEIGHBOUR
I have come to ask for a bit of fire for my Christmas stew.... It's very chilly this morning.... Good-morning, children, how are you?...

TYLTYL
Fairy Berylune, I could not find the Blue Bird....

THE NEIGHBOUR
What is he saying?...

MUMMY TYL
Don't ask me, Madame Berlingot.... They don't know what they are saying.... They have been like that since they woke up.... They must have eaten something that wasn't good....

THE NEIGHBOUR
Why, Tyltyl, don't you remember Goody Berlingot, your Neighbour Berlingot?...

TYLTYL
Why, yes, ma'am.... You are the Fairy Berylune.... You're not angry with us?...

THE NEIGHBOUR
Bery... what? Goodness gracious me!...

TYLTYL
Berylune.

THE NEIGHBOUR
Berlingot, you mean Berlingot....

TYLTYL
Berylune or Berlingot, as you please, ma'am.... But Mytyl knows....

MUMMY TYL
That's the worst of it, that Mytyl also....

DADDY TYL
Pooh, pooh!... That will soon go; I will give them a smack or two....

THE NEIGHBOUR
Don't; It's not worth while.... I know all about it; it's only a little fit of dreaming.... They must have slept in the moonbeams.... My little girl, who is very ill, is often like that....

MUMMY TYL
By the way, how is your little girl?...

THE NEIGHBOUR
Only so-so.... She can't get up.... The doctor says that it's her nerves.... I know what would cure her, for all that. She was asking me for it only this morning, for her Christmas box; it's a notion she has...

MUMMY TYL
Yes, I know; it's Tyltyl's bird.... Well, Tyltyl, aren't you going to give it at last to that poor little thing?...

TYLTYL
What, mummy?...

MUMMY TYL
Your bird.... It's no use to you.... You don't even look at it now.... And she has been dying to have it for ever so long!...

TYLTYL
Hullo, that's true, my bird!... Where is he?... Oh, there's the cage!... Mytyl, do you see the cage?... It's the one which Bread carried.... Yes, yes, it's the same one, but there's only one bird in it.... Has he eaten the other, I wonder?... Hullo, why, he's blue!... But it's my turtle-dove!... But he's much bluer than when I went away!... Why, that's

the blue bird we were looking for!... We went so far and he was here all the time!... Oh, but it's wonderful!... Mytyl, do you see the bird? What would Light say?... I will take down the cage.... (He climbs on a chair and takes down the cage and carries it to the NEIGHBOUR.) There, Madame Berlingot, there you are.... He's not quite blue yet, but that will come, you shall see!... Take him off quick to your little girl....

THE NEIGHBOUR
Really?... Do you mean it?... Do you give it me like that, straight away and for nothing?... Lord, how happy she will be!... (Kissing TYLTYL) I must give you a kiss!... I fly!... I fly!...

TYLTYL
Yes, yes; be quick.... Some of them change their colour....

THE NEIGHBOUR
I will come back to tell you what she says....

(She goes out.)

TYLTYL (after taking a long look around him)
Daddy, mummy, what have you done to the house?... It's just as it was, but it's much prettier....

DADDY TYL
How do you mean, it's prettier?...

TYLTYL
Why, yes, everything has been painted and made to look new, everything is clean and polished.... It was not like that last year....

DADDY TYL
Last year?...

TYLTYL (going to the window)
And look at the forest!... How big and fine it is!... One would think it was new!... How happy I feel here!... (Going to the bread-pan and opening it) Where's Bread?.... I say, the loaves are very quiet.... And then here's Tylo!... Hullo, Tylo, Tylo!... Ah, you had a fine fight!... Do you remember, in the forest?...

MYTYL
And Tylette.... He knows me, but he has stopped talking....

TYLTYL
Mr. Bread.... (Feeling his forehead) Hullo, the diamond's gone!... Who's taken my little green hat?... Never mind; I don't want it any more.... Ah, Fire!... He's a good one!... He crackles and laughs to make Water angry.... (Running to the tap) And Water?... Good-morning, Water!... What does she say?... She still talks, but I don't understand her as well as I did....

MYTYL
I don't see Sugar....

TYLTYL
Lord, how happy I am, happy, happy, happy!...

MYTYL
So am I, so am I!...

MUMMY TYL
What are you spinning round for like that?....

DADDY TYL
Don't mind them and don't distress yourself.... They are playing at being happy....

TYLTYL
I liked Light best of all.... Where's her lamp?... Can we light it?... (Looking round him again.) Goodness me, how lovely it all is and how glad I feel!...

MUMMY TYL
Why?...

TYLTYL
I don't know, mummy....

(A knock at the front-door.)

DADDY TYL
Come in, come in!...

(Enter the NEIGHBOUR, *holding by the hand a little girl of a fair and wonderful beauty, who carries* TYLTYL'S *dove pressed in her arms*.)

THE NEIGHBOUR
Do you see the miracle?...

MUMMY TYL
Impossible!... Can she walk?...

THE NEIGHBOUR
Can she walk?... She can run, she can dance, she can fly!... When she saw the bird, she jumped, just like that, with one bound, to the window, to see by the light if it was really Tyltyl's dove.... And then, whoosh!... Out into the street, like an angel!... It was as much as I could do to keep pace with her....

TYLTYL (going up to her, wonderstruck)
Oh, how like Light she is!...

MYTYL
She is much smaller....

TYLTYL
Yes, indeed!... But she will grow bigger....

THE NEIGHBOUR
What are they saying?... Haven't they got over it yet?...

MUMMY TYL
They are better, they are mending.... It will be all right when they have had their breakfasts....

THE NEIGHBOUR (pushing the LITTLE GIRL *into* TYLTYL'S *arms*).
Come along, child, come and thank Tyltyl....

(TYLTYL, **suddenly frightened, takes a step back**.)

MUMMY TYL
Well, Tyltyl, what's the matter?... Are you afraid of the little girl?... Come, give her a kiss, a good big kiss.... No, a better one than that.... You're not so shy as a rule!... Another one!... But what's the matter with you?... You look as if you were going to cry....

(TYLTYL, **after kissing the** LITTLE GIRL **rather awkwardly, stands before her for a moment and the two children look at each other without speaking; then** TYLTYL **strokes the dove's head**.)

TYLTYL
Is he blue enough?...

THE LITTLE GIRL
Yes, I am so pleased with him....

TYLTYL
I have seen bluer ones.... But those which are quite blue, you know, do what you will, you can't catch them....

THE LITTLE GIRL
That doesn't matter; he's lovely....

TYLTYL
Has he had anything to eat?...

THE LITTLE GIRL
Not yet.... What does he eat?...

TYLTYL
Anything: corn, bread, Indian corn, grasshoppers....

THE LITTLE GIRL
How does he eat, say?...

TYLTYL
With his beak. You'll see, I will show you....

(He moves in order to take the bird from the LITTLE GIRL'S *hands.* *She resists instinctively; and, taking advantage of the hesitation of their movements, the* DOVE *escapes and flies away*.)

THE LITTLE GIRL (with a cry of despair)
Mother!... He is gone!... (She bursts into sobs.)

TYLTYL

Never mind.... Don't cry.... I will catch him again.... (Stepping to the front of the stage and addressing the audience.) If any of you should find him, would you be so very kind as to give him back to us?... We need him for our happiness, later on....

CURTAIN

www.bookjungle.com *email: sales@bookjungle.com fax: 630-214-0564 mail: Book Jungle PO Box 2226 Champaign, IL 61825*

The Codes Of Hammurabi And Moses
W. W. Davies

QTY

The discovery of the Hammurabi Code is one of the greatest achievements of archaeology, and is of paramount interest, not only to the student of the Bible, but also to all those interested in ancient history...

Religion   **ISBN:** *1-59462-338-4*   **Pages:**132
   MSRP $12.95

The Theory of Moral Sentiments
Adam Smith

QTY

This work from 1749. contains original theories of conscience amd moral judgment and it is the foundation for systemof morals.

Philosophy   **ISBN:** *1-59462-777-0*   **Pages:**536
   MSRP $19.95

Jessica's First Prayer
Hesba Stretton

QTY

In a screened and secluded corner of one of the many railway-bridges which span the streets of London there could be seen a few years ago, from five o'clock every morning until half past eight, a tidily set-out coffee-stall, consisting of a trestle and board, upon which stood two large tin cans, with a small fire of charcoal burning under each so as to keep the coffee boiling during the early hours of the morning when the work-people were thronging into the city on their way to their daily toil...

Childrens   **ISBN:** *1-59462-373-2*   **Pages:**84
   MSRP $9.95

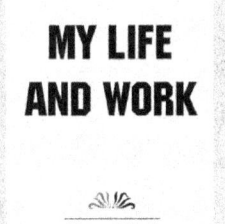

My Life and Work
Henry Ford

QTY

Henry Ford revolutionized the world with his implementation of mass production for the Model T automobile. Gain valuable business insight into his life and work with his own auto-biography... "We have only started on our development of our country we have not as yet, with all our talk of wonderful progress, done more than scratch the surface. The progress has been wonderful enough but..."

Biographies/   **ISBN:** *1-59462-198-5*   **Pages:**300
   MSRP $21.95

www.bookjungle.com *email: sales@bookjungle.com fax: 630-214-0564 mail: Book Jungle PO Box 2226 Champaign, IL 61825*

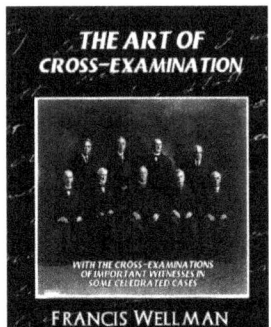

The Art of Cross-Examination
Francis Wellman

QTY

I presume it is the experience of every author, after his first book is published upon an important subject, to be almost overwhelmed with a wealth of ideas and illustrations which could readily have been included in his book, and which to his own mind, at least, seem to make a second edition inevitable. Such certainly was the case with me; and when the first edition had reached its sixth impression in five months, I rejoiced to learn that it seemed to my publishers that the book had met with a sufficiently favorable reception to justify a second and considerably enlarged edition. ..

Reference   ISBN: *1-59462-647-2*   **Pages:412**
MSRP $19.95

On the Duty of Civil Disobedience
Henry David Thoreau

QTY

Thoreau wrote his famous essay, On the Duty of Civil Disobedience, as a protest against an unjust but popular war and the immoral but popular institution of slave-owning. He did more than write—he declined to pay his taxes, and was hauled off to gaol in consequence. Who can say how much this refusal of his hastened the end of the war and of slavery ?

Law   ISBN: *1-59462-747-9*   **Pages:48**
MSRP $7.45

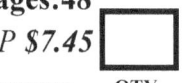

Dream Psychology Psychoanalysis for Beginners
Sigmund Freud

QTY

Sigmund Freud, born Sigismund Schlomo Freud (May 6, 1856 - September 23, 1939), was a Jewish-Austrian neurologist and psychiatrist who co-founded the psychoanalytic school of psychology. Freud is best known for his theories of the unconscious mind, especially involving the mechanism of repression; his redefinition of sexual desire as mobile and directed towards a wide variety of objects; and his therapeutic techniques, especially his understanding of transference in the therapeutic relationship and the presumed value of dreams as sources of insight into unconscious desires.

Psychology   ISBN: *1-59462-905-6*   **Pages:196**
MSRP $15.45

The Miracle of Right Thought
Orison Swett Marden

QTY

Believe with all of your heart that you will do what you were made to do. When the mind has once formed the habit of holding cheerful, happy, prosperous pictures, it will not be easy to form the opposite habit. It does not matter how improbable or how far away this realization may see, or how dark the prospects may be, if we visualize them as best we can, as vividly as possible, hold tenaciously to them and vigorously struggle to attain them, they will gradually become actualized, realized in the life. But a desire, a longing without endeavor, a yearning abandoned or held indifferently will vanish without realization.

Self Help   ISBN: *1-59462-644-8*   **Pages:360**
MSRP $25.45

www.bookjungle.com email: sales@bookjungle.com fax: 630-214-0564 mail: Book Jungle PO Box 2226 Champaign, IL 61825

QTY

	Title	ISBN	Price
☐	**The Rosicrucian Cosmo-Conception Mystic Christianity** by *Max Heindel*	1-59462-188-8	$38.95
	The Rosicrucian Cosmo-conception is not dogmatic, neither does it appeal to any other authority than the reason of the student. It is: not controversial, but is: sent forth in the, hope that it may help to clear...	New Age/Religion Pages 646	
☐	**Abandonment To Divine Providence** by *Jean-Pierre de Caussade*	1-59462-228-0	$25.95
	"The Rev. Jean Pierre de Caussade was one of the most remarkable spiritual writers of the Society of Jesus in France in the 18th Century. His death took place at Toulouse in 1751. His works have gone through many editions and have been republished...	Inspirational/Religion Pages 400	
☐	**Mental Chemistry** by *Charles Haanel*	1-59462-192-6	$23.95
	Mental Chemistry allows the change of material conditions by combining and appropriately utilizing the power of the mind. Much like applied chemistry creates something new and unique out of careful combinations of chemicals the mastery of mental chemistry...	New Age Pages 354	
☐	**The Letters of Robert Browning and Elizabeth Barret Barrett 1845-1846 vol II** by *Robert Browning and Elizabeth Barrett*	1-59462-193-4	$35.95
		Biographies Pages 596	
☐	**Gleanings In Genesis (volume I)** by *Arthur W. Pink*	1-59462-130-6	$27.45
	Appropriately has Genesis been termed "the seed plot of the Bible" for in it we have, in germ form, almost all of the great doctrines which are afterwards fully developed in the books of Scripture which follow...	Religion/Inspirational Pages 420	
☐	**The Master Key** by *L. W. de Laurence*	1-59462-001-6	$30.95
	In no branch of human knowledge has there been a more lively increase of the spirit of research during the past few years than in the study of Psychology, Concentration and Mental Discipline. The requests for authentic lessons in Thought Control, Mental Discipline and...	New Age/Business Pages 422	
☐	**The Lesser Key Of Solomon Goetia** by *L. W. de Laurence*	1-59462-092-X	$9.95
	This translation of the first book of the "Lernegton" which is now for the first time made accessible to students of Talismanic Magic was done, after careful collation and edition, from numerous Ancient Manuscripts in Hebrew, Latin, and French...	New Age/Occult Pages 92	
☐	**Rubaiyat Of Omar Khayyam** by *Edward Fitzgerald*	1-59462-332-5	$13.95
	Edward Fitzgerald, whom the world has already learned, in spite of his own efforts to remain within the shadow of anonymity, to look upon as one of the rarest poets of the century, was born at Bredfield, in Suffolk, on the 31st of March, 1809. He was the third son of John Purcell...	Music Pages 172	
☐	**Ancient Law** by *Henry Maine*	1-59462-128-4	$29.95
	The chief object of the following pages is to indicate some of the earliest ideas of mankind, as they are reflected in Ancient Law, and to point out the relation of those ideas to modern thought.	Religion/History Pages 452	
☐	**Far-Away Stories** by *William J. Locke*	1-59462-129-2	$19.45
	"Good wine needs no bush, but a collection of mixed vintages does. And this book is just such a collection. Some of the stories I do not want to remain buried for ever in the museum files of dead magazine-numbers an author's not unpardonable vanity..."	Fiction Pages 272	
☐	**Life of David Crockett** by *David Crockett*	1-59462-250-7	$27.45
	"Colonel David Crockett was one of the most remarkable men of the times in which he lived. Born in humble life, but gifted with a strong will, an indomitable courage, and unremitting perseverance...	Biographies/New Age Pages 424	
☐	**Lip-Reading** by *Edward Nitchie*	1-59462-206-X	$25.95
	Edward B. Nitchie, founder of the New York School for the Hard of Hearing, now the Nitchie School of Lip-Reading, Inc, wrote "LIP-READING Principles and Practice". The development and perfecting of this meritorious work on lip-reading was an undertaking...	How-to Pages 400	
☐	**A Handbook of Suggestive Therapeutics, Applied Hypnotism, Psychic Science** by *Henry Munro*	1-59462-214-0	$24.95
		Health/New Age/Health/Self-help Pages 376	
☐	**A Doll's House: and Two Other Plays** by *Henrik Ibsen*	1-59462-112-8	$19.95
	Henrik Ibsen created this classic when in revolutionary 1848 Rome. Introducing some striking concepts in playwriting for the realist genre, this play has been studied the world over.	Fiction/Classics/Plays 308	
☐	**The Light of Asia** by *sir Edwin Arnold*	1-59462-204-3	$13.95
	In this poetic masterpiece, Edwin Arnold describes the life and teachings of Buddha. The man who was to become known as Buddha to the world was born as Prince Gautama of India but he rejected the worldly riches and abandoned the reigns of power when...	Religion/History/Biographies Pages 170	
☐	**The Complete Works of Guy de Maupassant** by *Guy de Maupassant*	1-59462-157-8	$16.95
	"For days and days, nights and nights, I had dreamed of that first kiss which was to consecrate our engagement, and I knew not on what spot I should put my lips..."	Fiction/Classics Pages 240	
☐	**The Art of Cross-Examination** by *Francis L. Wellman*	1-59462-309-0	$26.95
	Written by a renowned trial lawyer, Wellman imparts his experience and uses case studies to explain how to use psychology to extract desired information through questioning.	How-to/Science/Reference Pages 408	
☐	**Answered or Unanswered?** by *Louisa Vaughan* Miracles of Faith in China	1-59462-248-5	$10.95
		Religion Pages 112	
☐	**The Edinburgh Lectures on Mental Science (1909)** by *Thomas*	1-59462-008-3	$11.95
	This book contains the substance of a course of lectures recently given by the writer in the Queen Street Hall, Edinburgh. Its purpose is to indicate the Natural Principles governing the relation between Mental Action and Material Conditions...	New Age/Psychology Pages 148	
☐	**Ayesha** by *H. Rider Haggard*	1-59462-301-5	$24.95
	Verily and indeed it is the unexpected that happens! Probably if there was one person upon the earth from whom the Editor of this, and of a certain previous history, did not expect to hear again...	Classics Pages 380	
☐	**Ayala's Angel** by *Anthony Trollope*	1-59462-352-X	$29.95
	The two girls were both pretty, but Lucy who was twenty-one who supposed to be simple and comparatively unattractive, whereas Ayala was credited, as her Bombwhat romantic name might show, with poetic charm and a taste for romance, Ayala when her father died was nineteen...	Fiction Pages 484	
☐	**The American Commonwealth** by *James Bryce*	1-59462-286-8	$34.45
	An interpretation of American democratic political theory. It examines political mechanics and society from the perspective of Scotsman James Bryce	Politics Pages 572	
☐	**Stories of the Pilgrims** by *Margaret P. Pumphrey*	1-59462-116-0	$17.95
	This book explores pilgrims religious oppression in England as well as their escape to Holland and eventual crossing to America on the Mayflower, and their early days in New England...	History Pages 268	

www.bookjungle.com *email: sales@bookjungle.com fax: 630-214-0564 mail: Book Jungle PO Box 2226 Champaign, IL 61825*

QTY

The Fasting Cure *by Sinclair Upton* **ISBN:** *1-59462-222-1* **$13.95**
In the Cosmopolitan Magazine for May, 1910, and in the Contemporary Review (London) for April, 1910, I published an article dealing with my experiences in fasting. I have written a great many magazine articles, but never one which attracted so much attention... New Age/Self Help/Health Pages 164

Hebrew Astrology *by Sepharial* **ISBN:** *1-59462-308-2* **$13.45**
In these days of advanced thinking it is a matter of common observation that we have left many of the old landmarks behind and that we are now pressing forward to greater heights and to a wider horizon than that which represented the mind-content of our progenitors... Astrology Pages 144

Thought Vibration or The Law of Attraction in the Thought World **ISBN: 1-59462-127-6** **$12.95**
by William Walker Atkinson *Psychology/Religion Pages 144*

Optimism *by Helen Keller* **ISBN:** *1-59462-108-X* **$15.95**
Helen Keller was blind, deaf, and mute since 19 months old, yet famously learned how to overcome these handicaps, communicate with the world, and spread her lectures promoting optimism. An inspiring read for everyone... Biographies/Inspirational Pages 84

Sara Crewe *by Frances Burnett* **ISBN:** *1-59462-360-0* **$9.45**
In the first place, Miss Minchin lived in London. Her home was a large, dull, tall one, in a large, dull square, where all the houses were alike, and all the sparrows were alike, and where all the door-knockers made the same heavy sound... Childrens/Classic Pages 88

The Autobiography of Benjamin Franklin *by Benjamin Franklin* **ISBN:** *1-59462-135-7* **$24.95**
The Autobiography of Benjamin Franklin has probably been more extensively read than any other American historical work, and no other book of its kind has had such ups and downs of fortune. Franklin lived for many years in England, where he was agent... Biographies/History Pages 332

Name	
Email	
Telephone	
Address	
City, State ZIP	

☐ Credit Card   ☐ Check / Money Order

Credit Card Number	
Expiration Date	
Signature	

Please Mail to: Book Jungle
PO Box 2226
Champaign, IL 61825
or Fax to: 630-214-0564

ORDERING INFORMATION

web: *www.bookjungle.com*
email: *sales@bookjungle.com*
fax: *630-214-0564*
mail: *Book Jungle PO Box 2226 Champaign, IL 61825*
or PayPal *to sales@bookjungle.com*

Please contact us for bulk discounts

DIRECT-ORDER TERMS

20% Discount if You Order Two or More Books
Free Domestic Shipping!
Accepted: Master Card, Visa, Discover, American Express

www.ingramcontent.com/pod-product-compliance
Lightning Source LLC
Chambersburg PA
CBHW081225170426
43198CB00017B/2711